Inquiries: curator@KeysDiscovery.com

ISBN: 978-1-0872-1709-3

Florida Keys History and Discovery Foundation
Post Office Box 1124
82100 Overseas Highway
Islamorada, Florida 33036

Forward

It was a different way of life in the Florida Keys when Jack and K Wilkinson made their home in a tent along Key Largo's Atlantic shore. Known as Tavernier today, the area had once been home to a farming community known as Planter. For the benefit of all of us, K Wilkinson understood the importance of her story when she began asking friends and family members to record their memories of those early years.

The Florida Keys History and Discovery Foundation was thrilled when Lindy Roth, friend of K's and holder of the original manuscript, allowed us to recreate this particular peek into a way of life in the Florida Keys that has certainly been lost to history. With the approval of K's daughter Katharine, "It Had To Be You" is being republished by the Foundation for a new generation to appreciate.

K was many things to her Upper Keys community including a member of the Daughters of the American Revolution and former president of the Historical Preservation Society of the Upper Keys. Katharine "K" Luisa Wilkinson passed in 2003 at the age of 87. Because of K's affiliation and support of the American Cancer Society, a donation from the sale of each book will be given to the ACS in her name.

The Florida Keys History and Discovery Foundation

It Had To Be You

Acknowledgements
I would like to thank the many people who helped me in this project. Without their assistance it could never have been completed. Pat Havel suggested the name and cover for my book and her choice was really an inspiration for me during the writing. Fran Williams and Karen Strobel worked with me from the beginning, transcribing tapes I had recorded of my memories of the tent days. They started me on the drive to get the job done. Thanks to Jerry Wilkinson for the story of a Conch Christmas and to all the old friends who contributed their memories of the wonderful times we had together. In alphabetical order, not their order of importance: Evelyn and Alice Allen, Dorothy Carey, Janice Parker Gentry, Marie Goecke, Marie Klink, Mary H. Lennox, Tookie Russell, Ann Tyrell and the Thompson brothers. Special thanks to Marian Hirsh who was my coordinator, advisor, computer expert and super helper in all phases of this story. I could not have done it without her—I love you, Marian!

Prologue

This is not just one story, but many as told by the people who lived it. Their memories take us back to the days when life was simpler, but not easy. It is a history of the paradise they found and the changes their coming made to the land. This is a story of the beautiful Florida Keys, the people in a community named Tavernier, and the family and friends of "K" Wilkinson, a lady whose work and devotion helped to shape the future and make the Keys what they are today.

Introduction

"If you're ever going to see me again it will be down here," were the words he wrote in the letter. I had decided, but how to convince my mother and family? How was I going to travel there? Most important, what was in store for me?

It was an uncertain future. We were living in a lean-to with no conveniences, few neighbors, lots of mosquitoes and little else. But, there was love and that was all that mattered. And so, as they sang in my favorite song, "It had to be you" Jack, "wonderful you." ... and I was right.

K. Wilkinson

K and Jack on the love seat – their first piece of furniture washed up on their shoreline.

Planter: An Early Key Largo Settlement
By "K" Wilkinson

In 1866, Captain Ben Baker, a wrecker from Key West, established a pineapple plantation on Key Largo. A few years later more settlers arrived, including Amos and Eliza Lowe and the six Johnson brothers. Lowe homesteaded 146 acres near what eventually came to be known as the settlement of Planter. By 1891, Planter had seven farms, a chapel, post office, a general store and piers.

A typical day for these "Conchs" included a hearty breakfast of bacon, eggs, grits, coffee and fruit, if available. The men worked on the pineapple plantations or fished, while women and children (when not in school) worked in the gardens.

Before the railroad, the only way to get to Key West was by an overnight boat trip. For those unable to make the trip (which usually occurred each week), the settlers made lists of necessities for their neighbors to buy for them. A usual list included a case of corned beef, canned roast beef, condensed milk, evaporated milk, salt, pepper, beans, sugar and flour.

Although there were wells at Planter, the water was sometimes too salty to drink. Well water was used for washing and watering gardens. Cisterns supplied the settlers with drinking water when there was enough rain.

A devastating hurricane ruined the pineapple crop in 1906. Another struck in 1909 and destroyed many homes. The population dwindled; the pineapple business was declining. Even the completion of the Over-Sea Railroad to Knight's Key in 1909 did not restore the town, and the post office moved to Tavernier in 1911.

Marvin and Victor Thompson subdivided Planter in 1925 and named it Palma Sola. But, the hoped-for land boom did not materialize and their development dreams were not realized.

The 1935 hurricane took its toll on the town and many moved from Planter to Tavernier. Three of the Thompson brothers, Marvin, Robbie and Anthony, chose to stay in Planter. They lived off the sea and had a little garden that took care of their needs.

In 1936, Jack and "K" Wilkinson came to Planter and lived on the shoreline in a tent for the next five years. Two children were born there, one in 1938 and another in 1940. They were raised on seafood and home-grown vegetables. Drinking water came from Tavernier and kerosene lanterns lit the night.

When World War II came in 1941, the Thompson brothers went to Key West to work in the Navy Yard. Jack Wilkinson was drafted, so "K" and the children moved to Coral Gables. The only people in Planter were Lillian and Chet Tingler, week-enders from Miami, who had a room built over a cistern. By the end of 1942, Planter became just a happy memory for those who had lived there.

Reprinted from the Monroe County Environmental Story

Johnny hauling in a big one.

In The Beginning

I first came to the Keys with my mother and family after my mother and father were divorced. He was just a great guy and a wonderful father. He went back to Quito, Ecuador, where he was born and raised. While he was married to my mother we lived outside of Philadelphia and many lovely people were entertained in our home out on the mainline. I could never understand why my mother and father broke up. As the years went by I realized that he could not compete with my great-aunt, who absolutely spoiled my mother to death. The competition was too great and unfortunately we never did get to see my father again after he returned to Quito in 1934. It just broke our hearts, but we were too young to realize what was going on.

My mother and I came to Coral Gables. She had a very good friend who said, "You must go to Florida. Miami is a very charming place and you will love it." Sure enough, she came down and she did love it. My grandmother was there to watch over the three kids so my mother came home and just raved about Florida, saying she was going to move there. She was an only child and did not want to leave her folks in West Philadelphia so we got them all packed up, sold their house, and came to Coconut Grove.

We had many lovely times there with my grandparents, but my grandfather was really very unhappy. He had a job in Philadelphia that he was promised he could come back to if he didn't like it in Florida so that was in his mind. I guess the climate and the relaxed way of living was not the way he was raised. He just didn't like Florida and my mother felt badly about that.

In the meantime, I had made some friends and they were very anxious for me to meet a man they felt was someone I would get along with well. They took me to meet him and we went down this rocky road in Coconut Grove along the Coral Gables canal to the waterfront. There was Jack, relaxing in his lounge chair,

Coconut Grove canal leading to Jack's camp April 1934.

with a little sip of his 'shine, listening to beautiful music coming from across the canal. I believe the people who lived over there owned one of the airlines. Someone was playing the organ and the music was just so beautiful and very comforting.

Jack had his little lean-to and a canoe and he would go out in the bay and catch crawfish and fish; he had quite a nice living right there. He was very disappointed in his job with Pan American where he had been a grease monkey for three years. After graduating from the Massachusetts Institute of Technology in 1931, he was unable to find a job. It was during the depression and he had searched everywhere, including New York and Canada. His father was determined he was to be an engineer.

When he came back to Miami, he got the job with Pan Am and after three years he felt he had earned a raise. He didn't get it and he wasn't going to wait around anymore so he just quit. He parked on this canal, fortunately, I guess, because when I look back, it was love at first sight. I thought this was great—he had everything he needed.

His father was still living in Havana. His mother owned a lot of property in Hollywood and Miami and was living in Hollywood at the time. She was very upset about the way he was living after the way he was raised and been provided with such a wonderful education.

We went back to see Jack many times and my mother finally invited him to have a meal with us because she felt sorry for him. In the meantime, he could fix anything that was wrong in the house so she felt she was paying him back by feeding him because he would not take any money. We had a swimming pool there that we all enjoyed, including my sisters Tookie and Carolyn, and my brother.

After a year, my mother couldn't stand having my grandmother and grandfather so unhappy so back to Pennsylvania we went. We were not there long when I received a letter from Jack saying that a good friend of his, Saylor Watson, was going to take him to the Keys where he always wanted to be. In the good old days, when he was going to Miami High, he had wonderful times fishing with his friends in the Keys when they could get past the old Card Sound Bridge and through all the mosquitoes.

We corresponded back and forth and it wasn't long before I received a letter saying if I wanted to see him again this is where he would be. Otherwise, he didn't know what he was going to do after a certain time. Of course, this upset me because I knew by now that he was the person I would like to be with. We had had many good times. He would take me out in the canoe and we'd catch crawfish. Just being out on the water in that kind of an atmosphere was very exciting. I had always said I wanted to camp out and it looked like that was the way it was going to be if I was going to stick around here.

I don't think my mother actually realized how I felt about coming to Miami in the first place. I was 19 years old, all of my friends were up north, and I was very lonesome. When I did meet some people in Coconut Grove and they wanted me to meet Jack it sounded fine with me. My two sisters were going to school there so they had other friends, but I was kind of left out. What was I going to do? Get a job? I had finished high school and there was no money for college or anything, so that was one reason that, to me, Jack was a very exciting person who had a lot to offer.

When he wrote and told me he was going to go to the Keys the first thing I said to my mother was, "Well, I am going to go." I didn't know how—I didn't drive, or have a car. It wasn't too long before she was convinced that I was going to get there, someway. She decided she would drive me down and we got a friend to go with us so she would have company driving. It was a long way to drive alone, but she was a spunky lady who could do anything. It was kind of exciting for her, too, to get back to Florida because she loved it so much. We drove down and made arrangements to meet Jack at the old post office in Tavernier—and there he was, waiting.

He was afraid to have my mother drive her car over the old road because it was so rocky and all the branches would scratch her car terribly. He decided that we would go up to Gene Lowe's road and he borrowed a skiff and that's how we got out to Planter. Thank heavens the weather was decent and we didn't get rained out. Of course, my mother had no idea what to expect. Here we had our suitcases and everything and putt-putt, out we went. To me it was getting very exciting.

We got to the dock and it was in pretty good shape. Jack, being a beachcomber, didn't let anything go to waste. Every piece of board that came up he would salvage and knock out the nails, straighten them out, and use them again to add another section.

Before it was finished, he had a dock that extended out 350 feet. He could always catch fish off the dock.

We unpacked and, fortunately, a friend of Jack's had a cistern, cottage, more or less, a little way up from his tent. They used to come down on weekends and had it fixed up real neat, with a double bed on pulleys that they could pull up out of the way. Down in the cistern they had shelves for all of their staple goods and whatever they needed for their weekend visits when they would come down and have parties. It was fun seeing other people and if the weather was bad we could go there and Mother and I had someplace that was a little more comfortable.

After about two weeks, she decided it was time for us to go back home. I said, "I'm sorry, but I'm not leaving."

She said, "Well, why not?"

I said, "I have nothing to go home to—I know I will miss you all, but I'm going to stay here. I'm in love with Jack, and I like this kind of living. I've had all the fancy business I want and I've always wanted to camp and by golly, this is my chance."

She said, "He doesn't have a job."

I said, "That's too bad, but that's his problem, not mine."

She said, "What are you going to eat?"

I said, "There's a big ocean out there and I love seafood."

It just seemed no matter what she said I had an answer for her and she knew I was not going home. Yet, she was not going to leave me there not married. So, after some discussion she decided to drive us to Ft. Lauderdale where we were married by a Justice of the Peace. What was so cute was that on the way home at 36th Street, where International Airlines was located in those days, not big like it is now, we stopped at a little barbeque place and that was my wedding breakfast. It sure tasted good. She drove us back and left with doubt in her mind that this was just a fantasy of mine and that I wouldn't hang in there very long. This was in January of 1937.

Good fishing!

For many months I wrote to her, telling her how I was enjoying the outdoors and learning all the things that Jack did, fishing, turtling, and crawfishing. Just being away from everything without the hustle and bustle that I was raised in was such a welcome change. Not only that, but I was with the person I loved. The mosquitoes never bothered me—it was just one of those things. In July of that year she finally announced we were married. She told people at the time that I was just visiting. It wasn't too long before the family decided that they would come to Florida. This is how I started my life in the tent. It lasted five years, until Jack was drafted.

After my mother left and I was there with Jack alone we would cook outside most of the time, mostly fish. We had no transportation. We would beachcomb and everything we found was used. Jack left me on the dock to sun and went back and forth on the shoreline and found this Nassau dinghy. He hauled it back and got some cotton that he could stuff into the cracks. The next day he walked to the hardware store for a big pole and that was what we used to get around. We had that for some time and it's surprising how you can do things when you have just a minimum.

He had all the answers. No matter what it was he had an answer so I never questioned anything he did or said because he knew better. He was smarter than I ever was. He must have been smarter, because he convinced me that this was the life he wanted and he was happy that I could be there with him. We would beachcomb and get many things that washed up; in fact, our first piece of furniture was a love seat. We had that outside and we'd sit in it and just relax and sun. It was a very pretty piece of furniture— where it came from, who knows. It's surprising the number of things that were thrown overboard from the boats, the big ships that went by and even from the yachts. The things they did not want—off they went, and when they reached our shoreline we picked them up.

We weren't in the lean-to very long before Jack decided it was time we got a bigger home. Up the shoreline was a big house that had belonged to one of the old settlers and had been there for many years. He would salvage the good lumber and haul it back and that is what he used for the floor. One time he was hauling some of this lumber and he took off his shorts while he was in the water. All of a sudden he let out a yell and I ran out to see what was wrong. An octopus had grabbed him by the balls. He was frightened, and he jerked that thing off as fast as he could, got back in the boat and to the dock. That was the last time he wandered around without any clothes on when he was going up the shoreline to get wood.

He brought the wood, laid it out to dry, and then started using it for the floor. The lumber was very solid so we never had to worry about falling through after he completed it. He built about an 8 x 12 room. For the sides he bought clapboard from Tavernier and put that up about three feet all around the outside edge of the floor. From there up there was an open space with a ledge at the very top that was about three or four feet wide. It was hitched on to the clapboard and that's what he put the screen and netting on. On the inside, the ledges were wide enough to hold anything I needed. At the back of the tent was a long shelf that had a two-burner stove.

We got a tent from Sears Roebuck and it was held up by a mast from a schooner that had washed in. It kept the tent up and we folded it over along the side where the tent could be rolled down or up depending on the weather. It was very clever the way he had it fixed up and you can't imagine it unless you see a picture. When the weather was bad we'd let the sides down and anchor them at points outside where he had posts in the ground, so they wouldn't keep flapping up and down. When the weather was nice we could roll the sides up all the way around or on either end, depending on which way the wind was blowing.

Our ¾ cot was to the right side as you opened the door and at the end of that was a cardboard closet that we got from Sears where I hung the few things I had. On the other side of that there was a potty that Jack improvised for me and it was supposed to be for my use only. Across the back was the big shelf that held the two-burner kerosene stove and on the other end there was a little ice box that held a chunk of ice. We had a kitchen table that I got from my grandmother and believe it or not, I still have it—it's under the house that I'm living in right now, though no longer being used.

Opposite from our cot was space where we could put a cot in case we had someone stay and spend the night. After Johnny was born we took that down and that's where we had the baby crib. This was the beginning and it was so comfortable, you can't imagine. Jack swept it out every day. It was clean as a pin and everything was so handy. If the weather was bad we just stayed indoors.

Old truck a friend left for
us to use. April 1937.

Our original little lean-to was used for storage and it was called the "rain barrel." Jack got some tin and built a big box over the trailer and that's where we stored the extra things and my extra clothes that we couldn't put in the tent. We had such limited space it really came in handy, parked right behind the tent. Trees across the front protected us as far as water was concerned. People would bring us things and we'd put them in the rain barrel; it was very handy. Jack made everything so unique and comfortable and people couldn't get over how we had everything so organized. We wouldn't have made it otherwise, especially when the weather was bad.

Malaka, My Mother

I have to thank my mother for the life that I had in the tent at Planter, mainly because if it had not been for her I would not have gotten to Tavernier to meet Jack and start this beautiful life. It was unusual and something I am very grateful for today.

I think it has made a better person of me and really gave me a chance to raise Johnny, Katherine and later Robert in Tavernier, in an uncluttered life, down to earth, and it was clean and clear and just beautiful.

When my mother drove me to Tavernier to meet Jack and saw the tent and what a God forsaken place it was, she must have looked back on the days she raised us in Philadelphia with all the nice things we had and wondered what she had done wrong. We didn't want for anything, even though the last part of our life there was during the depression. She was so resourceful and she took such care of us that we did not know there was such a thing as the depression.

Her life had been so beautiful. She had an aunt who had money, who educated her and sent her to Europe every summer and taught her how to play the piano and violin. She had a beautiful voice and she entertained in her home when she had parties because my father was in the diplomatic services as a consul from Quito, Ecuador. He represented Ecuador to Delaware, Maryland, and Pennsylvania and signed for everything that went in and out of the Port of Philadelphia. I am sure many things ran through my mother's mind. Here we were in

Malaka, my mother.
A great gal!!!

this wilderness with nothing except the outdoors and no conveniences. It was just one of those things that happen—where did she fail? Why was I all of a sudden going to do a thing like this and leave her and the family?

13

The more we argued, the more I knew I was not going to go home and she knew that better than anyone. In the end, she took us to Ft. Lauderdale and she was the witness to our marriage. Mother was such a very dear lady and she was a worker—a scenario writer for Fox Movietone back in the good old days. She had an office in Philadelphia, and of course all these things made her the person she was. I'm almost sure she wondered where my mind was, apparently content to stay here with nothing except Jack. At that point, this was all I needed and all that I wanted. I was blissfully in love. It was one of those things she could not fight and we won.

It is remarkable that eventually she moved back to Coral Gables when we were settled in the tent. She ended up just loving the place more than I did and so did all of my family. They were all in love with Jack and the life that we lived; they were jealous of us because in their position they could not join us. However, we had them down many weekends, which was great for us because they brought us so many goodies we did not have access to. So our lives were fulfilled by this beautiful family and friends that we met through them, bringing us all the chicken, spare ribs and steaks and things we were not used to. We had all this fish, conch, crawfish and everything they couldn't get, so we really had a feast every time they came. Their coming was always welcomed and we hated to see them leave.

We had to leave the tent when the war came along. In 1968, I wrote to many of my friends and the family asking if they would be kind enough to write any of the memories of the fun times they had at Planter. Back then, I thought how nice it would be to remember those days. The more I was away from it, the more I realized that it was the most important part of my life with Jack and my children and how nice it would be to recall and share those memories with them. I hoped someday they would be as dear to them as they were to me and Jack. My mother was kind enough to write her memories and I would like them read just as she wrote them. I think you can see how well we adjusted and how we fit into the community. I think her words will express that to you.

That is why I am dedicating this chapter to her. She is the one I have to thank for being here in the first place, and driving me back to Tavernier. I could not drive in those days and I could not have gotten here without her help.

14

Mother's Memories

Mother of Kay Wilkinson and in-law to Jack, I have many memories of the Old Planter section, which is now part of Harris Park. We as a family from Ardmore, PA., a suburb of Philadelphia, came to Florida in the autumn of 1935. We knew no one, but it did not take long to know and gain a wonderful group of friends on the Keys, especially in Tavernier.

At first I was not in accord for my daughter Kay to start housekeeping in a tent. Jack was such a genius for making tent living convenient and livable, they really had it made. Of course, Kay and Jack had no car, so Jack walked into town to bring water and groceries and usually got a lift from his good pals. Most of the water was collected in large containers from the rain. Their two children, Johnny and Katherine, I think learned to enjoy Mother Nature as they daily romped in the tall grasses for all sorts of insects, butterflies and little shell creatures along the edge of the ocean rocks near the tent.

I can recall the McKenzies' owning and running the electric and lights went off at midnight… some days it was off and one could not iron any clothes. Where Doug's Grocery store is today was McKenzies' Drug and Sundry store and quite the meeting place to hash things over. I can recall Yvonne Brownfield working there behind the counter and keeping us in good spirits with her timely stories and jokes. I can also recall Harry Harris, a soda jerk in his present place of business, Harry's Bar. Harry was, and still is, a wonderful person to everyone… including some of the old timer colored folks who have since passed away. Yes, and there was colored "Racket" who had but one eye but he sure was a sincere worker and I'm sure everyone loved that soul.

Of course, we never can forget John-the-Dutchman. He was already in Tavernier when Kay and Jack first arrived—then the Thompson boys.

Hardly any open roads… just a few and the main highway just wide enough for two cars… busses did not run too often and as I recall maybe two a day from Miami to Key West and vice-versa.

One attraction owned and run was the Driftwood Hotel… that lasted several years and was quite the place for fine cooking and eating.

I lived in Tavernier with my mother soon after the Wilkinsons left the tent when Jack went into service in World War II. Kay and Mother and I lived together in a rented house across from the homestead of Capt. Roy Tracey. Mrs. Tracey was a Godsend there, taking care of the sick, administering medicines, as she was the only registered nurse on the entire Keys. She treated my mother often. That present homestead is now owned by the Sistrunks.

Kay Wilkinson was always active in the general welfare of the Tavernier community and gave four years gratis in helping Coral Shores School where it is today. I can recall the old school where but a handful of teachers taught several grades and Prof. Albury was the principal and teacher also. Beside this, we must give lots of credit to Harry Harris for Coral Shores School as it stands today. One must understand the Keys to love it as I, my mother and the Wilkinsons have over these many past years. Maybe we should call those years the Golden Ones, and have lived these many years to see how Tavernier has grown into a prosperous community. In these 33 years here in southern Florida, watching the growth, one can hardly realize what has taken place.

I can recall when the Wilkinson's lived in Planter, how Jack would row out from the shore to supply Marineland with all sorts of fish and ocean gems to be taken back to Marineland.

The PTA today is quite an institution. I remember in Tavernier many years ago when this hamlet had but a handful of people, and the school held sessions in the old clinic. Once a year, three old timers, one of whom was Frances Tracy, gave out fruit at the clinic to the children, and this was a so-called PTA gathering.

Kay Wilkinson, always trying to be a useful citizen, knew there should be something better in store for parents and teachers, and decided to seek information as to a proper organization with rules and regulations—a real PTA. Kay attended instructions somewhere in Florida (place I cannot recall) and returned to Tavernier, and, with the folks interested, formed a PTA—was the original organizer of the PTA and served as president several years until PTA of Tavernier was well established on its successful way.

Kay Wilkinson also interested herself in the American Legion Auxiliary and served a few terms as president. It always seemed Kay was wanted by everyone in Tavernier, and whatever she

16

tackled, she went far out for this community and made a huge success.

I remember the present Tavernier Motel in by-gone days as only a garage and shed where McKenzie stored lumber, then it later became a movie place where shows were given once a week. With time passing quickly it is now a fine and modern motel with every modern convenience including room service and air conditioning.

McKenzies' prospered and moved his original drug and sundry store across the highway where it stands today with additions of hardware and merchant stores, gas station, car repair shop, the ice house and selling car accessories and tires.

I venture to say the Johnsons, living on the old road about Doug's Grocery Store, were Kay's first friends—two lovely elderly people. Their son was quite interested in diving for silk sponges, and in passing that house years ago, the traveler could pick up a beautiful sponge which hung on a clothes line along the road.

Jack was most resourceful in comforts for Kay and the children, Johnny and little Katharine. His old Franklin sedan, which he inherited from his dad, Colonel Samuel Wilkinson, had all windows and completely protected from bugs and mosquitoes by fine screening… so installed that windows could be opened and shut with no interference from the screening. I venture to say this Franklin was the only one of its kind in those days when Tavernier held but a handful of people.

I can recall Jack taking us out in his boat to catch turtles. One time he actually dove from the boat, got on the back of a huge turtle, tied it up to attach the ropes to the boat and brought it ashore, where he placed turtles in a caged corral just at the end of the boat landing, a little distance from the tent.

Mosquitoes were pretty bad in those times, so Jack tacked cheesecloth to the opening of the tent, which prevented mosquitoes from entering. In those days one had to buy water, so you can imagine everyone carefully using the water and never being wasteful with it.

John-the-Dutchman was noted for his growing delicious Key tomatoes, and I might add a little bit of the barter system was used. We would supply John and he, in turn, supplied us with tomatoes.

Did I hear someone say, "How about keeping clean bodily and showers?" Well, we did have an answer to that—one would soap up nicely and take turns rinsing with rain water and even ocean water. The Wilkinsons always had a way to combat any situation— just had to ask them and they had good answers.

P.S. from "K"

You can see that these were precious memories to my mother. There were written 22 years ago, in 1968, and it is now 1990. That's why it is so important that I get going and get all these things taken care of. These memories are very dear to me and I know they will be to my children and grandchildren.

I often think of the many times my mother and grandmother would come down and the feast that we would have. They actually hated to leave and after Katharine was born and Jack would take Johnny out fishing, they had many a good time. My mother would always try to con me into letting Johnny come up and spend the weekend with her because he was such a smart kid, well, anyway, entertaining. He would tell them stories of going out fishing and he was only three years old, but could talk very, very well—so well that sometimes I was very reluctant to take him out in public. I never knew when he would express himself with a cuss word he learned so well from his father when they would go out fishing and lose a fish.

You can see that as I look back over the years, and most of my friends are gone, these memories are more precious than ever. My mother loved the Keys and my Jack possibly more than I did, but with the kids coming along she was fighting me because there were no doctors or anything, just living in the outdoors. It certainly proved over the years, with my husband loving the Keys and loving us so dearly, that we could not lose and it was too good to be true.

As we go along, so many other little stories come up. I am nearing my 75th birthday as I write this and I figure that before I lose too many of the memories I have I must record them. Hopefully, it will be entertaining to my friends and anyone else who cares to read them.

My mother was a dear lady and I can never thank her enough; she was very, very good to my family and my husband's family and we all just had a good time together. It was a real treat after we stuck it out and defied everyone. My kids say that we were the original hippies because we did as we pleased, we squatted, we weren't hurting anyone and Jack shaved every day and always had his hair cut. We didn't smoke pot, we didn't smoke anything; we had a drink now and then, which was normal in those days, but other than that we did our own thing. We just enjoyed that which floated up on our shoreline and we made use of it. Each day that came by we didn't know who would come and see us or what it would bring, but every memory is priceless. We can never live it again, but what is so nice is that we had it and we are now able to share it with you.

Mother
Beautiful woman who gave us birth.
> To us you are the greatest woman on earth.

You fed us well so we would grow strong.
> You taught us the difference between right and wrong.

You taught us to honor both parents and brother.
> You taught us to share and to love one another.

You taught us to pray, our God to seek.
> You gave us your strength when ours was weak.

You tried to protect us from life's falling rain.
> You gave us comfort and shared our pain.

You gave of yourself to all you knew
> You became more giving as older you grew.

You earned our love, our total thanks.
> You overlooked many years of our boyish pranks.

God hear your many prayers, each amen.
> Six sons grew up, they are finally men.

God showed us His love, our needs He knew.
> He blessed us with His best… He gave us you.

Richard LaMarra

March 22, '37

P.O. Box 454
Tavernier, Fla.

Dear Helen:

I received your letter and I sure was glad to hear from you, especially that it hasn't been cold up there this winter. You must have a job on your hands with two kids. Francis better quit fooling around, kids are plenty of trouble with little thanks and two are plenty in my estimation.

Well don't ask me how I did it or how I'm doing, but I got married the other day, some fun camping out and married. I thought that was all I needed to make life complete down here so I found someone who thought the same and bingo, I went and done it. Ft. Lauderdale, $2.50 and in five minutes it was done. Well, things are picking up a little. Before, I only had a small trailer and a couple of fishing lines and a frying pan. Now I have a wife, tent, stove, radio, etc. Not bad. We get along fine so I am not kicking. She's 21, blonde, 5 ft. 4, 127 lbs. and she loves me. Family of Philadelphia, Katharine Louisa Mata.

I got a letter from Nana saying Joe might be down for a stay in Miami. Let me know and I'll try and get to Miami on a Monday morning or a Sunday evening. That's the way transportation runs here.

Write when you get over the surprise and I'll send you an announcement when we get married in church. She is a Catholic.

Affectionately,
Your brother,
Jack

P.S. Don't broadcast this yet.

Saylor Watson

I have to tell you about Saylor Watson. He was Jack's dear friend from their school days in Miami and the one who hauled Jack to Tavernier and out to Planter. I guess if he were not around this life would not have started.

Watson was quite a gentleman, worked in the hotels over on Miami Beach and just loved to fish. It was one of his favorite

Saylor Watson, he loved birds as well as fish.

hobbies. He was delighted that he could help Jack haul his little trailer with his mattress and pots and pans. After they got all hooked up they were stopped in South Miami by the police and it scared the life out of them. They did not know what they had done wrong, but the police stopped them because they did not have a license on the trailer.

Meanwhile, they had stopped in Coconut Grove, where Jack always got his five dollars of 100 proof alcohol. That was what he fell back on in those days, and mixed it with all kinds of goodies. He had it between his legs and he was afraid the police might investigate to see what he had; maybe they would think it was water. Watson told him he was

hauling his friend down to Planter where he was going to live and they would not be pulling the trailer up and down the highway, so the officer was very kind and let them go.

Watson got him over the rough road into Tavernier, over the highway into Planter, and got set up. After Jack and I got married, Watson came down because he liked to fish. He always had a cot on the inside of the tent. Before they got the little cistern fixed up we would have our friends come and sleep in. The mosquitoes were so bad we could not let Watson sleep outside. He was fixed up in the cot and Jack and I were in the other cot. It was real close quarters, but when you have friends like that, you don't mind sharing.

He was always primping; he was just a real good looking kid. He was always combing his hair, having a drink, using his flashlight. Jack and I wanted to go to sleep. We had lovely music on and Jack told Watson, "Put that light out, we want to go to sleep." He paid no attention and kept on primping. Finally, Jack said, "Watson, if you don't turn that light out by god I will shoot it out of your hand." He didn't pay any attention, so Jack reached under the cot and got his .38 and shot the light right out of his hand. There was not a word the rest of the night! He knew when Jack said something he meant it! It was funny, but I was glad to get to sleep and so was Watson, and we never heard a word from him after that.

Over the years Watson was so dear and his friends and wife Jane would come down to visit. Watson just absolutely loved my little Katharine. When Jane became pregnant Jack would say, "You old son of a bitch, I hope you have twins." Would you believe it, when the time came they had twins. Watson always blamed Jack for putting it on him. He was a good friend and he would always bring us little things we were out of and could not get here. He enjoyed fishing and it didn't matter what kind of skiff we had or he brought his own fishing gear. Over the years he would enjoy the feast that we would put up, and his wife and kids dearly loved it. They even brought their nephews down.

Everyone enjoyed the hospitality or they never would have come over that rough road. That was really something.

They remember coming over the bush and rocky holes. It was miserable; once they got to the end they were congratulated for having made it. Then they were gifted with all the goodies we had, and just the good time of sitting around the fires at night. It was like we had the world to ourselves. So Watson is one of the people I would like to thank, because he was the one that got Jack started here and I will always remember him.

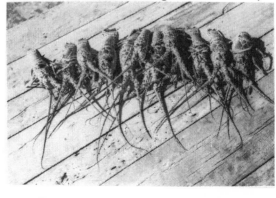

Typical seafood caught from our dock.

My Sister Tookie

When "K" decided to marry Jack it didn't seem to bother my mother too much, but I really think it bothered all of us. But that is what "K" wanted and she and Jack were very much in love, and that's the way it was.

I can remember going down there when they moved to Planter. You had to be very careful to find the right road as it was all coral and you had to be sure you were on the right one. I thought we would never get there; God, it was forever and you had to go about five miles an hour, just creeping because the coral was so bad on the tires. When we arrived, there they were, at the table outside. If there was no wind we had to hurry to get inside the tent and "K" would have to spray us so we didn't bring in the mosquitoes.

I remember going down on the dock and fishing. Once my friend from Coral Gables, Virginia Fox, came down with me for a weekend and we went over and slept in the cistern. In the middle of the night I woke up and said, "Virginia, something is crawling all over me." She said, "Me, too." We got a flashlight and looked and lo and behold, there were a million (maybe that's an exaggeration) scorpions! I couldn't believe it! We got up and out of there pretty damn quick and went down to the tent. We had to sit out on the dock 'till they woke up.

Tookie was sure a good fisherman.

Those are just some of the things I remember. I remember going out with Jack fishing, and him explaining how he used the glass bottom bucket. He threw out a little shark's oil and made the water smooth, and put the bucket down to show us. It was quite interesting, seeing how they trapped the fish, how they cut up the shark and how they cut turtle for turtle steak. That is the way it was in those days.

24

When we came down here we always brought a little of everything that we thought they could use because there was just a little general store. Our grandmother liked to come because she could sit there and they poured the moonshine into her. She got so high! She really enjoyed relaxing and having a great time. The moonshine tasted good and she thought it was a good treat regardless of the situation.

Jack would fill up different bottles with moonshine and put apricots in some, prunes in some, and raisins in some. After that permeated they were really like cordials. When guests came Jack would mix it with grapefruit juice, lime juice, or water and lime and it was very delectable. While you were drinking it went down real easy, but

Grandma loved her "toddy" when she came to visit.

all of a sudden it would hit you and you wondered what happened. That was one way he could serve moonshine without anyone realizing what it was and it was very smooth. Grandmother didn't do

Grandma Keifer (Mother's mother) always had the best seat in the house.

anything like that at home so she enjoyed it, as we all did. To drink it straight was pretty rough but mixing it with the different blends was like having a little liquor store. We'd say, "What would you like today? Apricot, prune, or raisins, or straight?" Everyone got a kick out of the refreshments and enjoyed the tent life without getting a hangover, and they usually spent the night so they kept out of trouble.

I was fortunate to be here at the time several trucks came down from Marineland Studios in St. Augustine. They would back up the trucks to the oceanfront and Jack had many pens out there with turtles, sharks, other rays, and small beautiful fish. They would bring their buckets and I would watch them load up the fish and put them in the trucks to take back. They would pay Jack for what they got and he would go out every day and look for different specimens they wanted. It was quite interesting to see. When we drove down one winter we stopped at Marineland and all I could think of was all of these specimens and fish that Jack had caught. I mentioned to them that my brother-in-law was one of the persons that helped get Marineland started by catching these things and I had seen the trucks.

One of the things Jack had to do in order to sell these fish was be sure there wasn't a mark on them. They had to be carefully handled and I never saw anything as clever as Jack reaching in with

*A good ride in our "super" boat was always a
treat with the family. Brother Jack, sister
Carol and Jack say Hi – K, too.*

tender, loving care for each of the fish, pulling them out delicately and transferring them from one place to another. The same thing that made the camp and tent so workable made his work with the fish possible. If you handled the fish too much you would scar them and they would die. The only thing they had trouble saving was the tiger or sting rays because they were hard to cage. They had to be tied out at the end of the dock and at night the sharks would come and take big hunks out of them, and of course they would die. That was one animal that was hard to load for them.

It is interesting that one of Jack's hobbies was fishing, which he adored, and here he was getting paid for something which was a real joy. So that worked out pretty well as far as finances were concerned.

Old Time Friends

I have had the privilege, as I look back, of interviewing, talking with and just having a fun time with some of the old Conchs. I guess you would say they are the people who settled the Keys; they have been called Conchs because there were so many of these shells in the waters around the Keys and the Bahamian waters, and they ate so much of the meat from this beautiful marine shell. At one time it was the staple food of the islands and they used it to make chowder, conch fritters, and conch salad. They had many uses for this wonderful food and it had so much food value.

I interviewed Myrtle Albury and Doris Albury (I think they are cousins generations removed) and they had so many stories, they were cute the way they would express themselves. They said they used the conch shells to communicate from island to nearby island and actually aboard ship to land and sea or ship to shore. It was one way for them to communicate and they had a very tricky way of putting a hole just in the end of the shell so that it would not hurt the shell itself. They would blow through it and it would let off an awful wail; it is hard to blow, believe me. It took a lot of breath to blow a conch shell. They would go to festivals and have the kids blow to see who could blow the hardest and loudest. They had all kinds of contests in those days and they would have to dream up things to do.

They went on to say that back in the Bahamas they were Tory sympathizers who left the Carolinas and they decided to reside on the islands; they would rather do that than participate in the American Revolution of 1776. All the stories that these ladies passed down through the years are so dear, I was happy to be a part of listening to them. The Tories said they would rather eat conch than go to war, so I guess over the years that's why they became known as Conchs. A real true Conch is a member of a very close knit group of these island people; they are really dear folks. They are very gracious, kind, clean living and witty, and they are God fearing people. Whenever you needed something they were right there to help you and do whatever they could.

Myrtle went on to say the Upper Keys go back about 120 years. Her father-in-law, Beauregard Albury, brought her husband Gene, his son, to Key Largo when he was only three-and-a-half weeks old, back in 1886. He lived in the family home in Newport in Key Largo. We remember Newport from years ago when I came here in the 1930s, so it is not new to many people. She said that Planter at that time had a one-room school house and students reached it in small skiffs and sailboats. If the water was rough they had to use a small path through the brush.

The period from 1905 through 1912 was the time the railroad was under construction and Beauregard's father supplied fish for the 1,100 men who lived in the ten or fifteen camps on the Keys. The fish were plentiful then. Lots of grunts, groupers, red snapper; sometimes they caught up to 1,500 pounds a day. They used only hand lines. They never had the fancy reels they have now, and they never used nets.

In 1910 lumber was $15 a 1,000 board foot and cement was .40 cents a bag; linseed oil was .40 cents a gallon. This was called Dade County pine, brought from Dade County, very tough and durable and hated by the termites because it was hard to chew through. Those of you who have experience in using Dade County pine know you often have to drill first before you can get a nail through it, so it was tough on the old termites. You can compare these prices with today's and you can really see the difference and how things have changed.

Beauregard's first car in Key Largo was a Model "T" Ford, probably a 1920 version. According to some records, Mamie Albury, her mother-in-law, ordered groceries from Key West by the weekly boat. I think it was called Richard Peacock's store. If she got seasick she had to rely on these services, so you can imagine those days by sailboat. For $25 she got a case of corned beef, a can of roast beef (I don't know how big those were), a case of condensed milk, a case of evaporated milk, some salt and pepper, beans, 100 pounds of sugar and a half-barrel of flour. Merle said Mamie was noted for her Key lime pie and especially her sweet potato bread. Many of the Conchs of today still make great pies and sweet potato bread.

Their big meal of the day was at noon. Supper was always served before dark because they retired early, rising at sunrise and ready for another day's work on the water, in their gardens and groves. They were very energetic and worked hard, so you know at the end of the day they were tired and ready for bed.

She said Beauregard and Mamie lived in Rock Harbor for 44 years and then moved to Tavernier in 1954 to be near their only daughter, Myrtle, who was married to Gene Lowe. Many memories are held dear of the completion of the railroad in 1912, the introduction of electric lights and the building on the Overseas Highway between 1923 and 1938 and the opening of the water pipeline in 1943. So, you see these folks remember all these things and it was so nice of them to share them with me.

I remember the first elderly people that I met were Tom and Ellen Johnson. They lived where the Driftwood Trailer Park is now. When Jack and I walked into town that would be our first stop, and they did not have very much. They lived on the sea fringe like we did, but they were always anxious to share whatever they had and insisted that Jack and I stay for a snack or if they were having fish (mainly boiled fish or fish stew). They knew the walk back to Planter was hot and long and wanted to make sure we had something in our stomach. Of course being dear folks they looked at us as grandchildren so I kind of felt quite at home. By that time I was getting used to the area and I was not as frightened of wondering what was going to happen. I knew the folks I was meeting were true Conchs and they just loved and admired us for the way we were living.

Tom Johnson was great; he could spear fish like you would not believe. You wouldn't think he could move because he had bad legs, but when he got out he would catch two or three fish. That was all they needed and they would fix it different ways—make fish cakes and boiled fish. Of course, they grew vegetables and their own lime trees, so when you look back there was not much that they wanted for. People would bring them guavas and they would make guava cakes for dessert.

The water was so precious that even to this day I cannot stand a dripping faucet. I am so conscious of it I go around turning them off; I can't believe the waste. They would use the water in the morning and then keep it until night. It was just thick, because they would do the dishes just once a day and none was ever wasted. When you look back to the way we live since then, the waste is frightful. Today you can see how important water is; Marjorie Stoneman Douglas stressed it in her writings. You can tell the folks back then knew that was sacred. They all had cisterns; when it did not rain they had no water. We had to buy ours for ten-cents a gallon and tote it in containers from McKenzie's. When we were on foot it was hard and we cherished it; it was very precious to us. I hope people realize this and listen to what the old timers have to say and take notes, and make it a better world.

Coleman Johnson, the son of Tom and Miss Ellie, was quite a sponger and I know that prior to the 40s sponging was quite a commercial industry. He loved to talk to us about sponging and he couldn't do very much. Of course, the weather had to be cool and calm and he would pole up and down the shoreline. He had a real long pole with a hook on it. They were called hookers; of course I don't think today it could be termed as such because they would be compared to something else. Anyway, it was a type of rake, and they would rake the sponges from the bottom. You could use this same type of hook to get conchs if it was too deep to dive for them or if you did not want to get wet. It was great to lift up a conch from the bottom of the ocean. He would tell us the buyers who would pay the highest prices for the Matecumbe. It was hard to get these sponges. They have a foreign chocolate colored residue and he would have to bang the sponges against the rocks to get all the excess water and residue out. Of course, there were a lot of weeds and shells stuck to them and he would have to pull them out, then string the sponges on a cord in bunches and hang them from the trees. When they were being cleaned and drained they could not be piled on top of one another, so after he got the worst out he would hang them in front of his little home. It was quite an attraction and as people went by they would stop to get their sponges. He had quite a story of the history of sponges and of course everyone was interested in what he had to say.

The sponges he had were beautiful. I remember Jack and I would go out and catch a few and we remembered how Coleman told us to clean them and make sure they were all right and how to get all the microscopic organisms out of them. We would then hang them up as he did, because it was important that they got the air and did not touch each other or they would be really sticky. He said that by 1940 about 90% of the Keys sponge crop had been destroyed and they were really few and far between.

Jack and Johnny – a WHOPPER!!!

Old Friends - Janice Parker Gentry on Planter

I met you for the first time "K" at a dance on FDR's birthday, in a house that had been either a grocery store or post office in Tavernier. I can't remember the year, but the date must have been

K loved the target practice we had and the fun hitting empty beer cans.

January 30 or 31. Jack asked me to take you to the restroom.

I saw the tent in its early years and used to go out there in that big old car with all the windows screened and the contents were a mixture of hardware and fishing tackle... even more than that. I always felt like we were "playing" house in the tent. You would do my hair and nails. You would prepare lunch. One day we had a fruit salad. It must have been good as I still remember it.

Yes, I did wonder why you would live out there in a tent. However, it was the most convenient place I have seen. You could sit at the table and reach anything you wanted, take two steps and be on the potty. It was so relaxing out at Planter and such fun just to be there. Those crawfish, conchs, and fish were so good. I was raised on seafood, but out there it was special.

I remember Johnny in his white training pants and white hair with a jar catching spiders, also sneaking some of everybody's wine until he was stumbling. Katharine was a doll. She and Johnny really enjoyed the wide open spaces. When the "bunch" would party out there at night, the kids were put to bed and no one was allowed in because of mosquitoes.

"K," my memories of Planter are very special and so are you. You and Jack were such gracious hosts. I enjoyed a lot of happy times out there.

A big jewfish struck off Tavernier Key.

An Early "Conch" Christmas

The majority of the early Upper Keys English settlers came from the Bahama Islands by way of Key West. Their families had settled in the Bahamas either directly from England, or were British Loyalists who left the United States after the Revolutionary War. Others had left when England ceded Florida back to Spain in 1784. Then in 1821, Spain ceded Florida to the United States. Being seafarers, the Bahamians slowly started migrating to Monroe County.

Around 1870, the sailing vessels were being replaced by steamships which did not wreck as often; so the "wrecking" business started to wind down in the Bahamas. It is said that one Bahamian in five left for the U.S., of which many ended up in the Florida Keys. The name "Conch" was attached to these early settlers probably due to the conch being used as a food and/or as a horn. Richard H. Russell came to Upper Matecumbe Key in 1854, followed by Richard Pinder in 1883. In 1866, Ben Baker grew pineapples on Key Largo, followed by William D. Albury in 1886. There were many, many more.

These early families relied on random sailing vessels to supply all their needs that they could not make, grow, salvage, or obtain from the sea. Key West was Florida's largest city and soon regularly scheduled schooners like the "Island Home" made trips back and forth.

Christmas was an important celebration for them. They were religious families coming from ancestors who fled England, enduring all kinds of hardships, primarily for religious freedom. In 1887, the Florida Methodist Conference sent down a circuit minister to rotate weekly between Key Largo, Tavernier, and Upper Matecumbe. Plantation Key built their church in 1899.

There were few or no pine trees in the Upper Keys, so the Spanish stopper tree was used. It was decorated with whatever was available. The meal was probably fish at first, until transportation permitted chickens and turkeys, which most families started raising for their own use. As difficult as it is for us to conceive, many vegetables were grown. Collard greens, sweet potatoes (a little stringy though), cabbage, tomatoes, onions (Bermuda), etc.

Presents were few at first, mainly clothes, but things improved as transportation improved. In early 1908, Henry Flagler had daily train service to Knights Key and Key West in 1912. A round-trip could be made to Key West in one day. Shopping lists were sent with anyone who made the trip.

As transportation improved, the stopper tree continued to reign. Toys started to appear—dolls for the girls and toy trucks, trains and tool sets for the boys and crayons for all. Almost everyone had chicken or turkey now for both Thanksgiving and Christmas. The Parkers even had a piano.

The first Overseas Highway opened in 1925. Cars, trucks, and busses could now regularly supply the families. Each key had at least one grocery store. Fruit cakes started to appear, even ice for homemade ice cream.

The 1935 hurricane set them back on their heels, but they recovered. In 1938, the highway was completed to Key West, but Miami now dominated. 1942 introduced public electricity and freshwater and the land boom was on. Excluding Key West, in 1940 there were 1,151 residents, and 53,192 in 1990.

My mother loved to watch and be part of all the activity – she's in the background not missing much.

Mother loved John-the-Dutchman and the tomatoes he grew and brought her, and of course the fish that Jack had for her to take home.

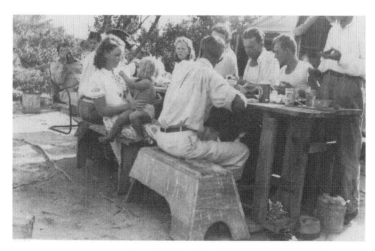

Mother always enjoyed our company and they enjoyed the extra goodies she always brought.

The Thompson Brothers

I guess the Thompson brothers were the first people we met, and they ended up being our dearest friends. They were the three brothers who lived back in the woods when we moved to Planter in 1936. Marvin Thompson was the middle fellow, Robbie was the oldest, and Tony the youngest. They were just wonderful people. What they went through in the 1935 hurricane and their life in Key West is really fascinating.

Marvin was quite the dreamer and a good storyteller, so as we sat around the fireside he would tell many exciting stories. Of course it was so new to me that I was full of questions. He told us he was born August 11, 1900 in the city of Key West and as a young man he went to work in the tobacco warehouse. His father owned the Thompson Cigar Company and it was one of the most important industries at the time. He stayed there for a while until he had an unhappy love affair and then decided to move to the Upper Keys in 1919, when he high-tailed it up to Planter. That is where he lived until the war started.

After the hurricane in 1935 his family would vacation in Planter; his father had bought 40 acres in 1918. Tony moved to Planter in 1924, but in the meantime Marvin was very interested in real estate and he decided in 1925 to subdivide the land in Planter. He called it Palma Sola. If you remember back to the good old days that was kind of the boom time. He had wild dreams that someday it would be a bustling community and he would build it up to have everything you would find in any other small town.

It did not turn out that way and the land boom went bust. He was appointed our first Justice of the Peace in 1927 by then governor John W. Martin, and continued in that position until 1934. Of course he had many stories to tell of this time of life. His brother Robbie was then the constable.

Five days after Pearl Harbor he went down to work in the U.S. Naval Station in Key West, in a supervisory capacity. He was very talented and knowledgeable in many areas. He worked and lived in Key West until 1946 and returned to the Upper Keys soon after he left the Naval Station. He told us about days past and his family and his father, who was so generous. He stayed in Key West and continued with the cigar factory, sending groceries up to the boys, though he didn't know what they were up to in Planter.

38

Of course they had to eat, and they had quite a nice garden. They grew tomatoes, okra, bell peppers and even rock melons, and they had wild coffee, wild tobacco and muddy tea, which they made from gumbo limbo trees. They also had clear tea, made from the

Madeira tree. There were so many things one could do with just what was there, people today cannot believe it.

When they got hungry they could fish, catch raccoons, rabbits and even

The Thompson Brothers: Robbie, Tony, and Marvin with K.

opossums. They had pineapple fields and their lime groves were fantastic. Today you hardly see a lime tree anywhere. But then everything was so plentiful, and you can understand why there was no reason for anyone to run out of anything.

The colored people would say they were going to Tallahassee, and this was the first time I heard this tale. Years ago we would talk about the Tallahassee Road and no one would know what we meant. When Marvin told us about the old folks I finally learned where and how this road got the name of Tallahassee. The workers had to carry baskets of pineapples on their heads around the lakes and creeks and over the planks across the swamps to the ocean side, to the ships at Planter. The main people who lived in Planter were on the shore of the Atlantic Ocean, and the owners quartered their laborers who worked the fields in a section by themselves near the water's edge.

All the produce was picked and transported to a small tram, which was railed to the wharf, where they were loaded on small boats or dinghies. In fact, it was a Nassau dingy that we refer to that Jack and I found, our first means of transportation when we went beach combing. They would be taken out to the freight schooners in the deeper water in Hawk's Channel and they would wait for the schooners to come and take them to the mainland. Working in the fields, the laborers would carry the pineapples in large baskets on top of their heads. They would go single file through the tangled jungle and walk a mile to the wharf. Part of the jungle was swampy. A weather-beaten narrow bridge, the heat, and the frightful mosquitoes made it very difficult for them. Each time it seemed long and their burden heavier.

They never traveled very far, but they had heard about this place called Tallahassee, the state capital, where all the laws were made, so far away it was almost to the end of the world. Trudging through trying to get their produce to the wharf one day, they said it was such a hard, long way that they were "going to Tallahassee." So from then on that road was called the Tallahassee Road, and whenever anyone got together to haul their stuff they would say they were going to Tallahassee to lighten their load, and it got to be a joke.

After Marvin completed his term as Justice of the Peace in 1934 they moved to Islamorada Beach for a year, and the youngest brother, Tony, had a radio station, W46J, in Matecumbe. Before the hurricane, Marvin went to the custodian of the veterans who were working on Flagler's railroad and told him that the storm was coming and to get the Vets out. The custodian was afraid if they went to Miami they would not get back, so he did not send them. By 4 pm the next day the storm was getting so bad they were told to go the railroad station.

When it started, the foreman told Marvin to get into the box car with the door open. After they got in the passenger train bumped the box car, spilling 55 drums of insecticide; you can imagine what a feeling that was. Then the tidal waves hit, and the whole car rolled over. He did not know what was going to happen. The deputy in the car had a gun and said he was going to blow his brains out. Everyone talked him out of it. They did not want all the blood around, and they felt that someone, somehow, would hear them and they would be found. They were trapped when the car rolled over and the water was coming up; they thought they were going to die.

They could see through the cracks and saw lumber blowing end over end. It was part of the barracks where the vets stayed. Finally, someone found them and passed a fireman's axe through the ventilator, and they cut a hole in the side of the box car. Being the smallest, Tony was able to crawl out. All he could see were bodies everywhere. It was a frightful experience, really a nightmare. The hurricane destroyed the electric meter service and everything was down.

After the hurricane, Tony and his brothers Marvin and Robbie were living in the big, old house in Palma Sola when Jack and I met them, and the house was in bad shape from the storm. The house was so crooked you thought you were on a ship when you walked in. They did not have any screens, but they didn't care. All they cared about, after going through that terrible experience, was black coffee, cigarettes, and kerosene for their lamps.

Since Jack and I were living in a sort of lean-to, they gave us one of their screen doors, and that is what we built our tent around. You can see we didn't waste anything. After a life that was so simple it was a new experience for me, knowing these guys had gone through so much. Nobody seemed to worry; they had no cares, no ulcers, no drug bills. You did not have to worry about lights or water. Well, the water we did have to worry about, because if we did not catch it in the cisterns, we had to buy it.

Every night we would build a big fire. Marvin would tell us stories about when he lived in Planter and Key West, and it was one way we passed the time. People would often wonder how we could pass the time, with the mosquitoes and the weather, because sometimes it would blow for three or four weeks at a time. We entertained ourselves by listening to these people, and we had a lot of good books. We were ardent readers so there was plenty to do, and it was a real treat listening to their stories.

I look back on those days that were so genuine and the memories are so dear to me, because so many of those folks are gone. Unfortunately, I did not take many notes. I never dreamed that I would be writing all of this, but Marvin, Tony, and Robbie were certainly very special.

When Tony grew older he worked in the Navy yard and he was a very talented man. He quit school when he was 12 years old and became a radio technician. He could do just about anything, but he was a loner. Often he would hide in the bushes when people came out after the hurricane, because he did not want to talk with anyone. He was a very good fisherman and used to catch a lot of the small fish for Theater of the Sea and at one time helped Jack when he did fishing for the Marine Studios at St. Augustine.

His life was very private, but he was quite a writer. He authored several poems and was helping to write a book about the Keys to preserve the history. He never got to finish his story as he became ill and went into a home in Key West. When you think about this, it was Tony's life when he lived in Planter with his brothers that was his contribution.

One of the last things that Marvin gave me, as he was also quite a writer, was an article printed in the Key West Citizen on March 6, 1967, The First and Last Trains, by Marvin Thompson.

Marvin Thompson, a great friend and neighbor up from our tent.

The First and Last Trains

By Marvin Thompson

That first time, most of the population of Key West was there, too. Thousands were milling about Trumbo Island and Pablo Beach, impatiently comparing watches as zero hour of the Great Day drew near.

Old Glory, the Cuban flag, and other banners, streamers and bunting waved in the breeze at every vantage point. The Light-Guard Band was in good melody, as was the ever popular "Phil Henson's Ragtime Family Band." Frankie Papy's entertainers always turned out when there was a need for special atmosphere and paraded with a martial air, flag flying, kettle drum rat-tat-tatting, base drum booming, led by Dad with his flute and wearing his Uncle Sam suit with red and white tails and high top hat with white stars in a field of blue. Always their rendition of "Yankee Doodle" was great.

Many tents had been erected on the man-made desert that was Trumbo for the comfort of the thirsty and hungry throngs. Baked ham and pork sandwiches were consumed as fast as the church ladies could turn them out. Wooden wine barrels filled with Key lime juice mixed with sugar, syrup and cooled with chunks of ice made a limeade that could not be equaled. Guava pie and fresh coconut ice cream also hit the spot. Other raters on the menu were turtle stew, crawfish enchilada and conch chowder, topped off with genuine Key lime pie.

Hordes of children accompanied their elders, all waving small American or Cuban flags and carrying bunches of roses and other flowers of many kinds and colors. Grandstand and bleachers resounded to their singing and laughing as they waited.

And now the atmosphere was rent by a sound such as Key West had never experienced before. It screeched and screamed like a trapped Everglades wildcat. It howled again from the swamps as it approached the Garrison Bight drawbridge, so that the bridge tender would make certain the span was safely closed. Finally, the huge black monster slowed the steady grind of its drivers and entered upon the bridge, bell clanging, clouds of steam spewing and spraying, black smoke belching.

The Light-Guard Band was giving out with "Dixie" as the first train to enter Key West rolled majestically into the station area. The mayor and other dignitaries were ready and primed on the speakers' stand, awaiting the arrival of Henry Flagler, the man who had just done more for Key West and Monroe County than any other person in history.

A final burst of escaping steam, a clutching of brakes, a clashing together of steel coaches, a last ding-dong from the bell, a valedictory wild cat screech from the whistle, and the black dragon snorted and slid to a stop.

The welcoming committee lined up where the great man would walk to the speakers' stand. A moment of hushed watching and waiting, and then, as a form appeared in the doorway at the platform, deafening applause broke out. Friends stepped up on both sides of Flagler and took his hands and arms in theirs. Steps with red carpeting were placed. The Grand Old Man paused, smiled and asked, "Do I smell roses?" Indeed he did, for children had strewn their bouquets along the path to the speakers' stand.

After Mr. Flagler had been graciously received by the mayor and other officials, celebration began on Trumbo Island, and elsewhere parades formed. As the day waned, the revelry waxed, and the quickened tempo spread to the Latin clubs. Their marimba bands formed a conga line in the city streets and swayed with the beat of the bongos. The club houses were gaily decorated inside and out with bunting and streamers, and the flags of both nations were displayed side by side as had been done for the many years since "El Grito de Yara," the clarion call for Cuban freedom. Steam whistles sounded at Consumer's Ice Plant, Columbia Laundry, and the power plant of Stone & Weber.

This was January 22, 1912, a great day in the history of the Florida East Coast rail line, of its builder, Henry Flagler, of the citizens of Key West, and of their neighbors to the south.

But now come along with me to the town of Islamorada, some 23 years later, on the night of September 1, 1935. Another railroad station, but no crowds. The weather was hazy and rainy, and there were occasional strong gusts of wind. Things had been seasonally inclement for several days, with intermittent rain squalls. The moon came out around sunset, through the dull gray curtain which the squalls had hung across the sky. Tomorrow night it would be full, a phase which mariners consider an omen of bad weather. (ED. NOTE: the moon would also be full during the lesser hurricane of 1948.) The palm fronds were threshing nervously and noisily.

A group of people had gathered with me at the station platform. The stationmaster was there, of course. Also, the telegraph operator, and the postmaster to receive incoming and ship off outgoing mail.

At the stops along the Keys, people waiting for the train would seek shelter in the station if it was raining, but when the engine sounded bell and whistle, they would rush outside, disregarding the elements. There was always the possibility that someone looking and waving out the window might be an acquaintance or perhaps an old friend come for a visit, mosquitoes and sand flies permitting.

This time when the train stopped, the porter, as usual, raised the metal flooring from over the steps; the conductor opened the door and preceded a lovely passenger who was getting off. She was very beautiful indeed and all aglow in spite of the rainy nights. An escort, her boyfriend, stepped forward to receive her.

A few other passengers came down the steps. The stationmaster exchanged greetings with the conductor, and mail pouches were transferred. The weather between Key West and Islamorada was discussed briefly, as well as the outlook. The ported signaled the all-clear. The conductor raised his lantern to give the high sign to the engineer. With a hard cough and spurt of steam the coaches began to roll slowly forward.

Who among those present could have known that he had just witnessed the arrival and departure of the last regularly scheduled passenger train on the Overseas Extension of the Florida East Coast Railway System?

It was Sunday, September 1, 1935, and the catastrophic Labor Day Hurricane was on its way.

Tony Thompson

This chapter is dedicated to Tony Thompson. He was a dear friend to Jack and a good fisherman. We would all go out turtling and getting specimens for the marine studios. When the war came along he left Planter for Key West and worked in a Navy yard for several years. Later he went into the old folks' home on Stock Island. He was the last one left in his family and there was no other place to go.

He had always wanted to write his memories and when he was gone his sister-in-law, Anna Thompson, gave everything he left to me. Among his papers were his notes about his days in Planter and they were very interesting. You can see what a nice guy he was. He was very private, but Jack was one person he got along with. They had many days out on the ocean together catching all kinds of things and he also contributed a lot of the small fish to Theater of the Sea. Although he was never able to finish his book, I want to acknowledge him for being such a good friend to us and share his memories with you just as he wrote them.

My Life
by Tony Thompson

Preface

My purpose for writing this book is to record the authentic history of the Florida Keys and the biography of their people for posterity.

Prologue

On December 24, 1913 I was born with scoliosis, a rare disease, better known as curvature of the spine. This disease disorganizes the patient's digestive system and eventually death will ensue from malnutrition. My stomach even refused to tolerate water and my doctor gave me up to die. The following morning, when my father was going to work, he met an old Cuban lady sweeping her sidewalk. She recognized my father and said, "Mr. Thompson, you look awfully worried this morning."

He stopped and related the condition I was in and she said, "I have two nanny goats at home and goat's milk is predigested and that will stay in his stomach and he will get well." She took one of her goats over to my house and showed my family how to milk it and they started feeding me goat's milk. I made a miraculous recovery. So by a miracle from God and the wisdom of the old Cuban lady, I successfully cheated death and lived to write this story, as it was told to me by my parents years ago.

During the most enchanting 50 years of my life I lived on the Florida Keys. My father owned a 40-acre bearing citrus grove at Tavernier and that was the most fascinating place that I ever lived. I moved to Tavernier during the summit of citrus season when the trees were loaded with tangerines, mandarins, grapefruit, oranges, lemons, and Key limes. This was the most spectacular display of fruit that I ever saw in my life, and to add to my already bewilderment, it was also the season to harvest melons and vegetables. I personally participated in helping to harvest this produce, which was my initiation for working on the farm.

Farming on the Keys was fascinating, but not very lucrative. The most dreadful phase of farming was having to ship your produce to the northern markets in hopes of getting a better price and having it freeze en route. I was victimized several times in this situation, and all that I received for my produce was a bill from the express company and a condemnation slip from the public health board. This is only one of the tribulations that the farmers were plagued with.

During my life on the Keys I have been exposed to both sides of the coin. I have observed the Arcadian beauty of the Florida Keys changing from season to season like a montage, and I have been intimidated with the impetuosity of tropical hurricanes that devastated communities overnight. The morning after a severe hurricane, the Keys are plagued by an epidemic of heartaches. While death and destruction haunt the shambled remains of each devastated community, the aftermath of a hurricane is very provocative to deal with. The water in your cistern is contaminated by the intrusion of salt spray from the ocean. Therefore you are obliged to set out containers and impound water from the rains until help arrives. During one of our Tavernier hurricanes, the Regal Beer Company of Miami anticipated our predicament and resolved our water problem. The next morning before our winds had mollified, the Regal Beer trucks were in Tavernier loaded with drinking water in quart beer bottles. This was a wonderful gesture on the part of that company and I have been extolling their virtues ever since.

47

The people of the Keys lived on whatever the natural resources provided. The menu consisted of a vast variety of seafood, raccoon, rabbit, squirrel, opossum, birds, land tortoise, land crabs, alligator, wild tobacco, wild coffee, and they concocted tea from the native teabush and the bark from the Madeira and gumbo limbo trees. The Madeira tea was reputed to cure kidney trouble, while the gumbo limbo tea was reputed to be an astringent and expedite blood clotting.

These people grew their vegetables, fruit, sugarcane, sugar apples, custard apples, guavas, avocados, coconuts, tamarinds, dates, papayas, soursops, Spanish limes, bananas, mangos, pomegranates, and there was an abundance of wild honeycomb for those who could muster the audacity to rob the bees. Whenever the people processed honeycomb, they retained the beeswax and amalgamated it with putty to make caulking compound, which was reputed to never crack under stress or desiccation.

Sapodillas are another delicious fruit that grows on the Keys. They are very popular among the Spanish people, therefore our best outlet was in Tampa. You can grow most anything on the Keys, but the cost of water is prohibitive for farming. When I first moved to the Keys we had lots of rain during the summer, but climatic conditions are different today and the Keys people have to buy their water. The Florida Keys aqueduct was one dye that cast the future of the Keys.

When I first moved to Tavernier, the object that fascinated me most was the post office. The building was a long and narrow wooden structure that was built close to the ground. In one end of the building was the post office and in the other end of the building was a small general store. In back of the building were two 50-gallon storage tanks. One of the tanks contained kerosene and the other tank contained white gasoline. I was overwhelmed by this situation. Never before in my life did I have to patronize the post office in order to buy kerosene and gasoline.

A short distance from the post office was the F.E.C. Railway Station. In the afternoon, when the northbound train was due from Key West, en route to New York City, the Tavernier people would meet at the railway station and wave to the passengers going through the train. This train was the Overseas Limited from Key West to New York City in 24 hours and it would pass through Tavernier like a bat out of hell and pick up the mail pouch without stopping. Occasionally, the arm on the mail car would default and rip the mail pouch open. Then the vacuum from the train would suck the mail up the tracks and the postmaster would be obliged to walk the tracks with a flashlight and try to recover the mail before the mosquitoes flew away with it. There was never a dull moment on the Keys and always a place to go for entertainment.

When I first moved to the Keys the only illumination that we had were kerosene lamps, lanterns, and candlelight. Then, later in progressive stages, we were introduced to carbide, gasoline and Aladdin lights. Those lights were a tremendous improvement over the lights we had been using. However, before we could retire nights, we were confronted with the custodial task of washing chimneys, trimming wicks, refueling lights, and replacing broken mantels. Life on the Keys has always been a surplus of problems.

Another one of the problems that plagued the Keys was the intrusion of flatirons for pressing clothes. These monstrosities had to be heated in pairs over a charcoal furnace, in order to always have one hot iron. The women referred to these as sadirons and the sad part came when you were requested to some pressing.

Death being a universal tragedy, the people on the Keys had to prepare to cope with it; each family retained, under their house, the material for building a coffin at the appropriate time. Whenever a death occurred, their paramount problem was excavating a grave in key rock. It was not always feasible to bury a person where you preferred. Sometimes you had to compromise and select a second choice. The Russell family on Matecumbe had a private cemetery of their own. They lived on a sand ridge; digging graves was no problem. During my activities on the Keys I was astonished to encounter so many graves on the Keys. On the north end of Key Largo most of the graves contain old settlers. Only a few of the graves have either a plaque or tombstone for identification, so who lies below is an idle question now.

In 1918 my father retired from the cigar manufacturing business in Key West and bought a 40-acre farm at Tavernier, Florida; 20 acres of the farm was a producing citrus grove, ten acres was a sapodilla grove and the remainder was coconuts, tamarinds, and dates. He paid $1,000 for the farm with two wooden houses, two concrete cisterns, two boat docks, one Nassau dingy, one packing house for processing the produce of the farm and one storage shack, which the rats and rattlesnakes were using for their convention hall.

All of my boyhood I wanted to live on an island and this was the answer to my desire. The day I arrived at the farm, I was bewildered. I wanted to explore everything at the same time. The Keys people were the most friendly that I ever met and it didn't take me long to start asking questions. During my first week on the farm one of my best neighbors died. He may have died from natural causes, but I think I talked him to death.

I received my education in the Key West Harris School and, living on the Keys, I was exposed to an education they don't teach in classrooms. When I first moved to the Keys the waterfront was still in the primitive stage, with very few people living there, so I took advantage of the opportunity and selected the most beautiful location on the ocean with an Arcadian setting, and built a shack. Whenever I had visitors they had to come by boat. I had a clear view for miles down the coast and if I saw someone coming that I didn't care to see, I walked back into the woods until after they left. There were a couple of pestiferous strangers that had nothing to do but annoy other people by the hour, so I made damn sure to hide from those people.

The day that I arrived in Tavernier the farmers looked to me like men from outer space. The shoes they were wearing had been re-soled from old automobile tire casings. Being inquisitive, I asked the farmers the purpose of these shoes. They laughed and replied that over the years the sharp-edged rocks on the Keys had been devouring the soles of their work shoes and that after many attempts to cope with this problem, this was the definitive answer. From my experience, the Keys have always been devastating to leather shoes. Whenever you walk through soggy seaweed, your shoes become permeated with salt and from then on your shoes are deliquescent, and will remain wet by absorbing the moisture from the atmosphere.

To rectify this situation, your shoes have to be washed in freshwater to remove the salt, then thoroughly desiccated in the sun until dry. The farmers worked under unusual pluvial conditions; the only time they were assured of having dry feet was after they got out of bed. Consequently, the farmers were plagued with athlete's feet. I am one of the victims of this fungus, and it's very violent to cope with. Every day your shoes and socks have to be fumigated, otherwise you recontaminate your feet. The dictionary defines athlete's feet as ringworms of the feet.

From my experience, there is a definite relationship between ringworm and beach sand. I am acquainted with several cases of ringworm that were on children who contracted it by playing in the beach sand. I don't know the origin of this fungus, but there is an affinity between it and beach sand. The farmers made a very effective fungicide: they saturated copper in a container of vinegar, then exposed it to the sun until it turned blue. Then everyday they soaked their feet and socks in this solution. I have observed the results from this fungicide and it's marvelous.

During the time I lived in Tavernier I decided to go into the Marine Curio Business. For advantageous reasons I selected the Planter waterfront for my base of operations. I needed a consistent supply of tidal water for keeping my specimens alive and that was the attribute that sold me on Planter. It was essential that I have a dock and keeping corral to operate from, and since the Keys are blessed with driftwood I went beachcombing to congregate the lumber that I needed for my enterprise.

I initiated this business by building the keeping corral first and from the inshore side of the corral I built my dock. The overall length of my dock was 110 feet and the width was modified by the lumber I used. At the conclusion of World War II I was the only person living at Planter, then gradually my friends came back. We decided to reanimate Planter from its moribund condition, so on weekends we organized beach parties at the Planter waterfront. During our parties everything was organized in a compatible manner. I agreed to do the cooking and my friends agreed to do the chores. My kitchen wasn't pretentious, but it was adequate and ventilated by the salubrious four winds of the earth.

I improvised my buttonwood stove from a few concrete blocks and a piece of expanded metal from my cooking grate. My bill of fare was naturally seafood, contributed by the ocean. Key legend has always reputed conch chowder as being an aphrodisiac for sexually jaded people, so whenever I cooked conch chowder it was the favorite of the Keys people. I agree that the chowder is delicious to eat, but my imagination is too thin to accept their philosophy. Regardless of what I cooked, it was a five gallon pot-full, which I thought would feed a multitude of people. But there were occasions when I had to cook two dozen crawfish to appease the appetites of my guests. After a full day of festivities at the waterfront, none of my guests wanted to accept the end of a perfect day and return home.

The Whispering Sea

The whispering sea had room for me,
To sail my little boat.
But the tide went down and left me aground,
So I cannot sail my boat.
Sometime soon the tide will rise,
And my boat will float again.
My little boat is just a float,
On this great big open sea.
So I study wide the change of tide,
So I can sail back to lee.
But the restless sea is good to me,
Yet it sometimes rocks my boat.
So I go shoreward bound to safer ground,
And anchor under the lee.
But never be on Neptune's sea,
When storm clouds are close around.

By Tony Thompson
Upper Keys Reporter
January 14, 1971

My Life Tonight

Tonight my thoughts are traveling
Far back into the past,
Thinking about this life of mine
As I travel from room to room.
I gaze around each room with care
And try to recollect,
The things that are, and the things that were,
But tonight I am a wreck.
My poor heart keeps throbbing
While I try to ease the pain,
And I wonder why this heart of mine
Keeps dying all in vain.
Tonight I am a vagabond
But tomorrow I shall rise,
And cross the bar of happiness
As I look into the skies.
I shall ask for God's forgiveness
To ease my heart from pain,
And never shall this life of mine
Be wasted all in vain.

By Tony Thompson
Upper Keys Reporter
February 18, 1971

Old Friends – the Allen Family

This chapter is dedicated to the Allen family. We became good friends after they came down to the Keys in 1939. Bob and Jack got along so well because they had the same ideas about nature and preserving everything they could. Bob was a research scientist for the National Audubon Society and he was sent down here to check on the roseate spoonbills and find out why their population was declining. He lived in a tent on Bottleneck Key, off the Tavernier Bay, and he was gone most of the week. We got together on weekends and had many good talks. He would tell us about his job and he was always interested in the fishing and turtling, often helping Jack when he had the time. It was a good change for him. The Allen family did so much in the community. Evelyn was a Julliard graduate and she did so much in the community and the school with her music. We were very happy to be with them and they enjoyed our tent life. Bob and Jack would have plenty of stories to tell, but they have both passed on and Evelyn and Alice have written about their memories of days past.

The Allen family enjoying the dock at Planter.

Evelyn Allen

One of the things I remember most was trying to get from the little U.S. 1, which was a two-laner with mangrove growing right up to the very edge, to "K"'s tent, which was about a mile. It seemed endless, and the car just swerved and bounced. There was no road underneath, there were just trees cut away so they didn't smack you in the face as you drove through.

I was a stranger in these parts at the same time that "K" and Jack were making their way. Bob and I had come with the Audubon Society and we had a job to do with the spoonbills. I was a musician. Having two little children and living in a trailer, I had to find something to do so I got busy with my music.

It was a wonderful thing to find "K" and Jack, who were really here with the same general idea that we had, accomplishing something on the Keys and making a life for ourselves. All of us came from an entirely different environment. I think one of the things I remember most is walking into their little camp and being impressed with the complete efficiency of the whole setup. I know now how organized "K" is, but I didn't then. Jack, of course, surpassed her many times, but there wasn't a thing they needed that somehow between the two of them they did not devise.

The tent was comfortable, you had everything you wanted; you never missed electricity or running water. Everything outside was in order, the dock was built, the boats were in good shape, the place was clean as a pin and tidy. "K" always looked like Mrs. Astor, Jack was always equally Mr. Astor. Not clothes-wise, perhaps, but fastidious about their surroundings, which made it

possible for them to withstand all the problems that do come with living like that and doing without things that you are used to having.

So, for my two little children and Bob and me, it was a real haven when we

Evelyn enjoying her time to relax and sun on our dock.

wanted to get away from all the problems of the spoonbills and trying to get around and get Bob out to his camp and my music started. It was a real haven for us to go out there and spend a day.

One of the most wonderful things of all was eventually they built a room on the dock, a screened-in room where we could literally take the children, open the door and toss them in, and lock the door. They had everything they needed in there, toys, food, water, and we could go about our business knowing the children were as well off as we were. It's wonderful when you have kids to have someplace you can literally toss them. We would run back and forth on the dock, checking on them and keep on doing the things you do when you can get rid of your children for a while.

One thing was the pleasure the children had together. Alice and Johnny were of an age and therefore delighted to find each other and indulge in whatever kids at that age do. One indulgence was almost fatal. We were just having a good time, enjoying ourselves and the breeze, and suddenly realized Johnny and Alice were not around. We went looking for them and they were not too far away. Johnny was painting Alice with aluminum paint that was used to paint the top of the tent to reflect the sun. She was standing so still and proud! They envisioned that she was going to ride an elephant in the circus. God knows what they must have been talking about and why they even thought to do it, but we caught Johnny painting the last part of her ear lobe. We all screamed and carried on.

We all grabbed what we thought was kerosene, but it was water and the more we rubbed Alice the more she screamed. She was in a fit, she was so mad that we were taking the aluminum paint off of her. Johnny was disappointed because this was a work of art. All the kids wore in those days were just little panties and even the panties were aluminum. She was solid, and it scared us half to death. When we realized it was water we hurried to get the kerosene and the poor child was bright red before we were finished. This is just the kind of once in a lifetime type of thing these kids got into and enjoyed so much. They were very smart and clever and they did the kinds of things most kids wouldn't even think about.

One of the most shocking things was my first evening in Tavernier. The nice people here had been alerted that the Audubon was sending a man to study the spoonbills and asked that they cooperate with us and do what they could. They were anxious to do that, so they invited us to a community sit-around and chat social, which was a nice thing for them to do. It was very hot and sultry in October, hurricane-type weather. We got ready to attend and I dressed my one-year-old daughter in her coolest outfit, a little pair of panties. We all walked up from our trailer behind the old hotel, which was also the theater, to the meeting place next door to the grocery story. The original grocery store was across the street from the original drug store, and this meeting place was where everyone met. It used be a school room. That more or less locates where it was.

We started up the little walk to the social; I looked down at my child and every square inch of her was black, literally covered with mosquitoes. Of course we were slapping them, but they had just latched on to her, being a sweet little tender-skinned individual. We hurried and got to the door and we couldn't see a thing inside of the meeting place. It was all screened with drop shutters for weather, but we could see nothing but smoke. When we got to the door he got the flit gun out and flitted us all and a man we later found out was Roger Albury.

We dashed into the building and spent the entire evening visiting with these lovely people, all native Conchs, not being able to see them or breathe because of the smoke from the smudge pots. There must have been a dozen of them. The people who were used to them were sitting there and talking and not seeing each other, but it was quite an experience for a city gal. This was our introduction to the social life of Tavernier, and I had plenty of opportunity later to learn to live with this, believe me. I burned smudge pots in my own place.

They were not running any pictures in the theater. I put on three different shows with Professor and Louie Pellicier, Mr. Doll and his wife, Leona Donaldson and all the original residents who were there. I had them all in the show. They didn't know how to dance. I had done a lot of playing in New York in dance studios and had studied dancing, so I taught them all tap dancing. We had minstrel shows. Prof was the Interlocutor and it was absolutely terrific. It was the only place that anything could have been happening, so it was just what I did there musically.

The drug store was a kind of meeting place where the bus would stop; it was the only social place and was a highlight of the early years. It was the center of everything. There was one old beat-up upright piano in the back. Of course I was immediately escorted to it the first time I walked into the drug store and from then on the music became a big part of Saturday night, the only time people did get together. We had some fine musicians from Key West, the very best Dixieland and swing. Jazz musicians who heard about the little set-toos we had up here came all the way from Key West just to sit in.

We had electricity; it came on at 6:30. Austin Reese ran the generator. Mac and Hazel owned the drug store at that time and Broomfield and Yvonne were the managers and they worked behind the counter. The generator was supposed to be turned off at 9 p.m., but if we played our cards right and we could get enough free beer from the bar we could sometimes get Austin to keep it on until midnight. We often did, and if we didn't we lit candles and went on playing the piano and our instruments and had our set-toos until three or four in the morning, or when we felt like stopping.

They were wonderful, wonderful times. Now that I think of some of these musicians who have gone on, and hearing about them over the years, I realize what a wonderful thing it was for me to have this outlet because I was pretty bereft otherwise of anything musical.

One other interesting thing was Bud and Marty McKinney arriving in Tavernier just about the same time we did. They were just as new as we were and they had just as many problems to solve as "K" and Jack and Bob and I did. We were all up against the same thing and wanted to get something accomplished, but how? They wanted to have this Theater of the Sea; I don't remember if that was the name that they hooked onto in the beginning but it was a good name. They had no idea if it would go over and did not know how they would get backing. They didn't know if anyone outside the Keys would be interested in loaning money to do this, or what kind of set up they could get that would be close enough for water and still not on the water, to be able to make ponds and canals to use for dolphins and such.

We would all sit there at one table, those little drug store tables with the little iron chairs with curlicue backs, with our beer, and it was wonderful. We would listen to Marty and Bud tell us about his dream, which now of course is the famous Theater of the Sea. It was interesting that it started right there.

I always remember the Franklin car. They would go out in it and go up to Tavernier. It was something else; you could find anything you wanted, it was like the store. Anything you needed, Jack would yell, "Just a minute, I have it in the car." He would go get it; he knew right where it was.

Alice Allen

Alice is the daughter of Evelyn and Bob Allen and she spent many a day out at Planter. She and my Johnny were great friends and she has many wonderful memories of the early life here. She related the treks to Miami and Homestead and tells us about those days. Her early days at Planter were when she was only three or four years old, so she can't remember many of them, but she can remember her early life growing up in Tavernier. I could not relate these great days any better than she did; our family was a part of all she recalls. Alice now teaches the grandchildren of her mother's piano students. Here are her words:

When we came to the Keys my father decided this is where he wanted to be. He would be out on the bay all week, leaving Mother on her own. It was a hard life for her. Water had to be carried up from the ocean just to flush the toilet. He never considered leaving here, but I bet she did every day. They quickly became a part of the little community. That community is still here, as are many of the Conchs and non-Conchs they met and befriended.

There was always something going on in our house. Biologists, botanists and writers were in and out constantly. There was no power until after World War II. Even then it wasn't full-time power; there were always interruptions because a bird sat on the wire. Water pipes were on top of the ground and a drunk would run off the road, and there was no water for a couple of days.

There was no air-conditioning. You didn't stay in the hot house, you went out in the evenings to catch a breeze to cool off and blow the mosquitoes away. We used a flit gun—remember those? We'd get flitted from head to toe and it was oily and slippery.

There was a little local store, but usually the big shopping was done in Homestead by "K" and Mother every two weeks and everything was put in huge freezers. Every meal was planned right down to the last slice of bread. All the fish, turtles and shrimp anyone could want were right there and the students often paid for lessons with fish.

The proximity to Miami was a godsend. There were no doctors or hospitals in the Keys until I was almost out of high school. My brother was a brittle diabetic so we made many emergency trips to Miami. Almost every Saturday all the kids would go by Greyhound bus to get to the dentist or doctor. When the appointment was over we could go to the movies.

It was wonderful being a kid growing up here. The water, woods, towns and families were an endless world to explore, constant learning. It was a very close knit, small town. There were only about 200 people living in Tavernier back then. I remember the town having a Christmas tree between the old and new highways, with a gift for every child. Everyone had his own present, with his name on it, and they were out there under the tree with no fear of anything being stolen. In those days, you never locked a door.

The old Tavernier school was above what is now the health building. One half of the building was grades one through six and the other side was everything else. Then, a portable classroom became grades six through eleven and the old building was divided into two sections. We didn't have to wear shoes until we went to Coral Shores so we went barefoot. I went there in the second half of the ninth grade and was in the second graduating class in 1954 with only 12 other children.

In the very early days the old Tavernier Hotel was the center of activity. The Conch families from the Plantation Key area would come and park their cars in front and listen to the music, but would never come in. We were the outsiders. After the war, the old drugstore had a bar and was the social center but the Conchs would still park outside and watch and listen, but never come in.

P.S. from "K":

Alice has been such a part of my family and I refer to her as my "surrogate daughter." She fills a void since my children and grandchildren live too far away to help me when I have a problem. Her memories are so dear to me and she told it "as it was" back then. "Tent days" with my son, Johnny, are priceless and important memories.

Turtles

I think turtling was one of Jack's favorite experiences here on the Keys. I don't know where he learned about it, maybe he did it as a kid in Miami or maybe when he came to the Keys, but he enjoyed it so much. After we got our little skiff he would pole into Tavernier and stop at Rodney Albury's before he walked to the post office to get a few groceries. They would reminisce and he learned a lot. Rodney remembered when the hawksbill, loggerheads and green turtles were plentiful in Florida Bay, especially in the area of Cape Sable. He told what it was like to go turtling at the turn of the century.

They would sail across the bay to the turtle feeding grounds off Cape Sable, arranging to arrive before dusk, then anchor and keep real quiet waiting for darkness when the turtles would gather to feed. They would feed on the bottom of the turtle set, as they called the feeding grounds. All the following day they would be busy getting the nets in place. The turtle nets were about 300 feet long by 15 feet deep, made of cotton twine in a diamond pattern. Twelve-

inch bars were fastened in each diamond to keep the nets extended and to aid in catching the turtles' flippers as they flopped in the mesh. Floats supported the top of the net and the bottom edge was held in place by bricks.

I remember so well watching Jack set the nets. As I look back I realize that all of the little things that Rodney told Jack were very important and he kept them all in his head. We would sit around the fire at night and he would tell me about all these things. Rodney said you have to be careful, a green turtle doesn't bite, but a loggerhead will bite the stuffing out of you. I remember that very well. Green turtles are faster and hard to catch. Loggerheads you can wear out. We did on many occasions.

Rodney remembered hunting for turtle eggs on Tavernier Key, a mile across the harbor from his home. On the sandy southern shores at just about the high water line, the females would dig a hole two or three feet deep and deposit their clutch of from 100-130 eggs. Then the ponderous marine reptiles would lumber slowly back to the safety of the sea. Rodney told us about his cousin Beauregard Albury chasing turtles by boat after motor boats became common in the Keys. He sought them out at the mouth of Tavernier Creek where Angelfish Creek meets Hawks Channel.

When the wind was right thousands of floating Portuguese man o' wars were swept in towards the shore and the loggerhead turtles could be found feeding on these poisonous purple jellyfish. The loggerheads would close their eyes to avoid painful stings from the fiery tentacles of the jellyfish. While they fed you could come in against the wind and the turtles would not be aware of the approaching outboards. They didn't hear too well and Jack would find out where they were feeding on the man o' wars so he could go there to try to catch one. Turtles have no external ears, but they have a keen sense of touch and can feel vibrations. Their eyesight is so good, too, and they can perceive colors. I know that when we were out hunting them they could see us and would get out of the way as best they could.

Jack always learned something about turtles along the way and I'd try to observe the best I could. It was such a great food, but the Conchs would hate to see them butchered. The loggerhead was preferred by the Conchs because it was a better taste than green turtles and I agree. They would grind up the meat like hamburger, all odds and ends of pieces from the steak, and make pretty good turtleburgers with garlic and onion in it. Or they would dip a slab of meat in batter and broil it, and that was very tasty, too. When you eat it this way it tastes like veal.

Sometimes when we went turtling we got more than we needed. Jack built what was called a turtle crawl not far from where the old Driftwood was. When we'd get two or three big babies in there they would fight. They would be all over the crawl from one end to the other and would come together in the middle with a "clack" that was like an explosion. It was a treat for people to come by and see them and it was one way we could keep them and not run out of turtle. When Jack was fishing for the Marine Studios in St. Augustine they would often want a turtle and we would get it for them.

Jack saved an article he'd had for many years and I dug it up the other day; I think it's worth repeating. The loggerhead marine turtles come ashore to nest from Florida to North Carolina. The endangered green turtle and leatherback turtles nest on the east coast of Florida. The shells of adult green and loggerhead turtles are about three feet long and they may weigh over 300 pounds. Adult leatherback turtles can be twice as large and I remember those we got were at least that big. The female comes ashore at night and will lay about 120 white leathery spherical eggs, covering them with sand. The same turtle may return at approximately 14 day intervals to lay several nests between early May and late August. Sea turtle eggs must remain undisturbed in the warm sand about 60 days before they hatch. After they hatch, the hatchlings remain in the nest

for several days to absorb their milk sacs. Many eggs are eaten before the catch can be born and come out.

Although female sea turtles lay thousands of eggs each summer, very few hatchlings survive to adulthood. They make their way out of the nest in a united effort and usually emerge at night to make their way down the beach and enter the surf. Some researchers believe that the crawl to the sea is important to find the proper course in swimming out to the sea. The race of the hatchlings from their nest to the sea is crucial. Lights near beaches will cause hatchlings to become disoriented and wander away from the sea. Many kinds of accidents befall sea turtles when they enter coastal waters. Some are caught on fishing lines while others are hit by boat propellers. Still others are caught and die in commercial fishing nets and others die from natural causes. Information gained from the study of such dead turtles may be important in developing ways of preserving future mortality.

Jack mentioned that the green turtle and loggerhead are turtles we can catch and are familiar with, but others we can't, such as leatherbacks, Kemp's ridley, hawksbill and the olive ridley. I had no idea there were so many different kinds of turtles. There are certain places you can get the others, but most you can get in the Florida Keys. We caught them for food and also to sell them. Other people had jobs and didn't have time to go out like we did. We had all day and half of the night if we wanted. Turtling was really a very important part of our tent days. When we knew we were going to have company we would try to have a turtle ready, but we had no refrigeration to keep them. We'd take them to friends in Tavernier who would keep them in their freezer. That helped a lot so we'd have one available for when we wanted to have turtle for dinner.

I guess what we did was a popular thing because a lot of the natives we became friends with were treated to things that they raved about in later days. When they got married and had families and had to work they didn't have time to catch turtle to have, so they always enjoyed coming out to see us. The Conchs are just real dear people and we made many nice friends. We enjoyed having them, and we had the time to make the effort. Besides, it kept me out in the sun, which I liked and it gave me a chance to work the little skiff. When we went out hunting turtles I had to be particularly careful not to jerk and throw Jack out of the skiff, but he was quite good at striking turtles. Sometimes it might take an hour to run a loggerhead down. Little green turtles are pretty fast, so we weren't too lucky in getting many of them.

Over the years Jack would clean out the shells and polish them up so when people wanted a souvenir they could have a turtle shell. We had a lot of them around, but little by little we got rid of them all. The last one deteriorated and now I don't have any, but I have my memories and that is what is important.

Turtles were a great part of our life at Planter – very exciting to strike them and then also trap them in nets – set off Tavernier Key.

The Carey Family

I visited with Dorothy Carey, who lives near Helen, Georgia with her daughter Marlene Sanders. She was kind enough to share some of her memories from when we knew them and when they came to the Keys.

She told us about the Carey house, which is a landmark in Islamorada behind the Green Turtle Inn. A pink concrete house with a lot of history, it was built in 1936 by Captain Everett Carey, her husband. She and her three daughters were survivors who lost family in the 1935 hurricane.

His dad, James Edwin Carey, of Bahamian descent, first lived in Key Largo and raised pineapples and other crops. After the harvest, the crops were brought to Key West by boat to the market place. This is where he met and married Clara Louise Thompson. As time passed they left Key Largo by boat and settled in Islamorada where their children would be closer to the only church and school, which is where Cheeca Lodge stands today.

They bought a large parcel of land from ocean to bay from the Green Turtle Restaurant to the next curve south, which is quite a beautiful piece of property. He built his wooden home directly on the beach along with a packing house and grocery store. Travel in those days was strictly by boat so you had to be near shoreline to avoid carrying articles too far. He also started a Key lime grove on the property. The place was occupied by eight Careys.

With the railroad running where U.S. 1 is today, a road was being built alongside. Mr. Carey decided to move his grocery store, now with gas pumps, across the street. There is a white two-story house there today. The old U.S. 1 ran in front of this house years ago. Up the road was the Rustic Inn, one of the few dining-out spots for travelers in the Keys. It is now the Green Turtle Inn.

We had many good times with the Careys and all of the friends who had children who went to Coral Shores. I remember so well the Green Turtle Inn, which it was called in 1946. Sid and Roxie Sideras had a bar, now San Pedro Trailer Park. I remember it so well because it was my first night out after Robert was born in September. It was quite a treat for me and I remember having to help them behind the bar. They were there for a while and then they moved to where the Green Turtle is today. Those are the days we remember and we always appreciate these folks sharing these memories with us.

Besides the Careys, there were the Parkers, the Pinders and the Russells. They were referred to as Conchs because of their Bahamian descent. On Monday, September 2nd, 1935 a hurricane of great magnitude hit the Florida Keys with the eye passing over Islamorada. On the oceanside there were eight Careys preparing for the storm, Everette's father, his two brothers Franklin and Charles, his wife and two children, Rose and Beverly, and their sisters Eloise and Ellen with her husband Lewis Moore. Everett and his wife were in Miami at the time, as was his mother; sister Rosalie was in Key West.

A long night would follow as local people braced for the storm that brought destruction to the islands. By morning, five of the Carey family would lose their lives in the awful tragedy. Everette's dad, his brother Charles, and his wife and two children would be lost.

It was sad that so many of these Keys folks lost so much and you can't help but feel bad every time a hurricane comes and you think of all those incidents. Those who survived were his sister Ellen Dolores Moore, who was found along the bayside in a hammock of trees about one mile away, and his brother Franklin and brother-in-law Lewis, who were located along the bay. Can you imagine being found like that? It is surprising that they did not lose their minds.

That 1935 hurricane was the end of the Flagler Florida East Coast Railway system between Homestead and Key West. Five hundred and seventy-seven bodies were found; the full total will never be known. Islamorada was completely flattened and stripped of its vegetation and trees. The railroad train on its way to Key West was tossed like matchboxes on the island. The track and rail twisted in configuration as a reported 17-foot tidal wave engulfed the island.

After the killer storm, the government, along with the Red Cross, decided to erect 20 or 30 homes built to withstand the rage and fury of another hurricane. They would be called hurricane-proof houses and would be given to the survivors who had lost family and belongings in the storm.

The houses would be made from poured concrete walls formed to be 12 to 14 inches thick, with a concrete roof, plate glass crank windows embedded into the walls, and a cistern for catching freshwater at the time. The Red Cross also handed out many other items and necessities to the local people.

Twenty-five years later, in 1960, Hurricane Donna raced through the Keys, hitting Islamorada dead center again. Millions of dollars of destruction would be done to homes and businesses, but all the hurricane houses remained intact.

Everette Carey sold the house to Mr. and Mrs. Belcher of Belcher Oil Company. They enjoyed it for many years as a weekend cottage far from urban congestion. Capt. Carey, one of the best known bonefishermen of the Keys, passed away in 1979. His love and devotion to fishing, along with his constant study of his quarry, ranked him at the top of his profession, never duplicated to this day.

The new owner, Capt. Ron Wagner, was also a bonefishing guide. He and his wife Carol worked hard to restore this quaint little home. They covered much of the state buying numerous items to bring it back to that period of 1936. Much love and devotion has been put into this restoration. They have named it "The Carey House" in honor of the Carey family who lived there. Besides, Capt. Carey's sister, Ellen Moore, who lived just across the street, would not want it any other way.

So anytime you are down that way, see the little pink house behind the Green Turtle Inn. The Carey House brings many memories to those of us who had the pleasure of meeting and enjoying the Careys and their family. I thank Dorothy for sharing these memories with me and helping me to remember the times we had with them in the 1940s.

Conchs

I guess you could call this chapter "all conched out." I never knew it would take this long to get my memoires together and to share the letters that my friends have sent me about what they remember of their days in the Keys.

One of the first things that I remember after we got settled in was "conking." I never imagined that I would ever eat any of those lovely animals and it turned out to be one of my favorite foods, as well as that of my kids. There was no problem finding conchs. The dinghy was very comfortable and we went up and down along the shoreline and got the conchs right in the shallows. We only took as many as we needed. The shells were absolutely gorgeous and when we got back to the dock Jack would break a little place on top of the shell without hurting it. With a sharp knife he would go inside to release the animal and then we would throw the shells over the dock so the little fish could eat out any meat we might have left.

After cleaning them, we invariably would eat them raw. We'd cut them and squeeze some lime juice, sometimes with just a slice or two of onion and it was really very tasty. That's how they made the conch salad that you might get in a restaurant. Then we would make a big conch chowder, which my folks just adored when they finally got to come down, and in fact everybody loved it. We would also have them ground up in conch fritters, which is a very

Jack goes out looking for conchs – has a special hook
on end of pole to get them out of the water.

popular way to eat them. Whenever the weather was nice we would go along the shore line and it was a nice ride. Of course, I always enjoyed the sunshine and it was an easy way to go around.

Many times when we were sitting out around the fire in the evening Jack would try to introduce me to all these things that I was going to face in the Keys. He just thought that a little education wouldn't hurt me. He would always joke if I did something stupid and call me a dumb son of a bitch and I'd say, "God damn you, you married me didn't you?" I guess he just wanted to make sure that I knew something about where I was living and the food I was eating. He would then save all these little goodies that he got out of books or newspaper articles he read and I would like to share them now because it kind of explains about the conchs.

The conchs come into the world as minute embryo eggs. They are tightly wound in strings of capsules that may contain up to one-half million embryos. Within five days the conch larvae, called beligers, hatch out and immediately begin moving up toward the surface. In this early stage of life they are able to propel themselves through the water by means of two minute wings called bella lobes. Once at the surface, they swim and drift with the ocean current for about three weeks, all the while feeding on plankton.

From the time they are hatched the beligers have very tiny shells called proto conchs. These minute shells continually increase in size and will eventually result in a large adult conch shell. When the baby conchs lose the ability to swim they settle to the bottom and the bella lobes are absorbed. At this time they begin to grow a foot for locomotion and also a mouth that will be used for feeing upon the algae that grows on the bottom. During the day the tiny juvenile conchs burrow themselves into the sand around the roots of the turtle grass. This is an instinctive action and it's done to avoid predators, for the baby conch has many enemies. At night they come out of the sand and feed on the films of algae that cover the blades of turtle grass and other fixed objects.

The conch has so many enemies that it is a wonder they ever survive to maturity. Crabs are probably their greatest menace, particularly in the first two years. The powerful claws of the crab can easily break away the lip of a young conch shell and pull the animal out. Hermit crabs commonly use conch shells, particular the small ones, as houses. Before the hermit crab can have his new shell house he must first evict the natural occupant and there goes another conch. Other conch predators are sharks, rays, skates, loggerhead turtles, groupers, tulip snails and crawfish, as well as octopus. An octopus den is frequently cluttered with conch shells of various sizes, most of them empty. The conch shells have been neatly drilled on the end so that the octopus can paralyze his prey and then easily remove the hapless conch from its shell. Once the pink conch has reached three years of age it is considered mature. Although the shell may grow slightly larger with age, the meat content will usually not increase measurably.

You can see from the little bit of information that I got from the articles that Jack gave me how really unusual these conchs are. I always think of this every time I eat conch and I feel badly about it as now there is a limit on the times and number of conchs you can take. Over the years there have been so many that people have just taken for their shells and thrown the meat away, which is just terrible. It's like most of the other things that they've had to limit. The conch is very popular now and still one of the foods that I just dearly love.

Old Friends – Marie Klink – Memories of Planter

My first visit to Planter was in '41 – Jack took me down to meet the rest of the family. The ride over that dirt and rock road was my first jolt! The dirt roads I was raised on were never like that! Then came the first glimpse of your car – with screens in the windows yet! Was that an old Packard? Or what?

Now we get to see the "tent." It was so hard for me to believe that people lived in a tent, with no electricity, and raised three kids there too! My idea of camping slanted to lodges and cottages. I had never been an "outdoorsy" type who liked to rough it. I tended to be the "hot house flower" type! For the longest time I really thought you were just "camping" and would go home one of these fine days.

Marie Klink with my brother Jack, she sure enjoyed this place.

I already knew Jack was a graduate of M.I.T. and it just didn't seem normal for you guys to be on permanent vacation! I remember the first time I saw Jack put the kids in the water and they swam like little fish! The first walk on those narrow planks out to the end of the dock! I wonder how come I never fell off that damn thing!

I remember little Johnny racing some kind of bugs, with lots of legs; he'd put them on the picnic table and race them, then he'd pull one leg off each and race them again! One was a bit faster than the other, and he said, "Look at that son-bitch go." And how old was he then, three or four?

I remember the time you and Jack were drinking the "dago red" wine and I told him you couldn't get drunk on wine! He made a bet with me that he could get me drunk on wine. We started early afternoon, and I remember sitting on that camp table about 4 p.m. and the next thing I knew I just fell off it! My Jack put me to bed and I woke up the next day with the worst hangover I ever had! Do you know I never took a drink of any kind of wine (not even champagne!) after that!

Do you remember the night I woke up, had to go to the "john," walked down the path to the "outhouse," dark as pitch, felt around for the hole, and sat down on one of the red-headed lizards! I let out a scream and came running back down that path, screaming my head off! Think I woke everybody all the way to Tavernier!

I remember one time when you and Jack took me fishing and I got a bite and got so excited trying to reel it in that my top slipped down around my waist and I didn't even notice it. Your Jack was laughing his head off and I thought he was laughing at my expertise with a fishing pole! Don't know how long it took me to notice my top was down!

Marie adored Johnny and Baby "K" and loved going to Tavernier in the screened-in Franklin car shown in the background.

I can remember us all piling in the old car and doing the town, from Harry's on up and down the road. I was trying to remember some of the folks we drank with. There was Bob and

Evelyn, can't remember Harry's wife's name, she didn't play with us very much anyway. There was Yvonne and I can't remember the name of the guy she married. Then there was that fisherman your Jack was always playing jokes on, like putting smelly cheese in his boots, etc. Who was Slim?

Do you remember the time I ran into the Highway Patrolman? We had been having a few at one of the bars on the bend in the road as you come into Tavernier, and some lady had been hit by a car as she crossed the road some place near the drug store. The patrolman left the bar for the scene of the accident and my Jack and I left after we finished our drinks. The patrolman stopped all cars, including ours. I was driving and he wanted to see my license; he was diverting traffic and I reach under my seat for my purse, and when I did I took my foot off the

Marie always enjoyed the fish we caught and helped to clean them.

brake and rolled right into the patrolman! My Jack yelled, the patrolman yelled, and I didn't know what I had done, since the guy was on his knees and I couldn't see him!

I remember sitting up in that crow's nest at the end of the dock and watching your Jack cut up a turtle. The first time I had ever seen that, and he took the heart out and it beat for a long time all by itself, just laying there on the dock! I didn't think I'd be able to eat it, but I did! I remember the first time you guys made conch chowder and I didn't think I'd like it, and I loved it! And Key lime pie! God, what I wouldn't give for a piece of that right now! I remember your Jack cooking up a batch of crawfish, melting a can of butter and we'd sit out there in the early morning and gorge on it!

I remember sitting out on the end of the dock and watching that full moon come up! We had such good times there, I never wanted to come back to town! Do you know these memories are over 40 years old? It was fun—and sad—and I'm glad you asked me. Love, Marie.

Sponges

According to some of the articles that I have read, sponging in the Keys developed quickly in the years following the United States' acquisition of Florida in 1821 and by 1849 the sponge industry had gained commercial importance. By 1900, the annual catch had a value in excess of $750,000.

I remember going out many times years ago to get a real sponge and we wondered why they were so rare. Now when I look back I can see why. To get these sponges and do it correctly you spoil them. When we were living in the tent we'd hear this putt-putt out on the water and they were out there getting sponges. They had a special hook and a pole and if the sponge wasn't the size they wanted or if it was a new little sponge they threw it back. That killed the whole thing. You really have to know how to do it and it's just a shame that now there are no real sponges anymore. The sponge's years were short lived. Cubans and Greeks crowded the Conchs near the shoals with no concern for prior right or conservation, plucking every sponge from the ocean regardless of size or quality and rapidly depleting the areas where sponges had thrived.

I know when Jack talked with some of the Conchs they remembered the days when top grade sponges were hooked all along the shoals of Key Largo, especially in Hawks Channel, a ten to fifteen foot deep cut that parallels the Keys just inside the fringing reef. One of the Conchs said that they would use the shallow draft boat because they would be able to scull slowly to a likely spot, then thrust a giant glass-bottom bucket over to see whether they were in the right spot. When they sighted the sponge, they would feel around the weeds and the debris alternated with patches of sand on the ocean floor and throw out a buoy to which a piece of lead was attached by a ten-foot length of line. This marked the sponge. Grasping a long pole tipped with a special hook, they would probe the bottom for the sponge and scrape it up.

I know Jack was so particular because of his experience in the Keys. He knew how to do it right. Over the years we looked out with our field glasses and could see people on the water and check out what they were doing. It broke our hearts and even though we reported it, it just seemed the people who were throwing the little ones away never were caught. That depleted our sponge industry, which is gone today. Now they have artificially produced sponges, but they are nothing like the real ones. When Jack would get several we would bat out all the dirt and stuff that was in the sponge and let it dry for a long time. Once it was dry there was nothing finer. We would have a bucket of water out so the sun would heat it and, with our sponges, go out to the end of the dock and sponge down. That was a wonderful way to shower and then just stand there and let the wind dry you. The real sponges are really worth something today.

In the early 1900s, Key West was considered the sponge capital of the world, furnishing 90 percent of all commercial sponges. In later years, overfished beds, along with blight and the introduction of artificial sponges, drastically reduced the trade. When we look back and remember when we could get our own, it was a real treat. I have not heard recently about anybody trying to get sponges and I don't think there are any left, so at least we had that experience.

Old Friends – Marie Goecke

To use a cliché, where have all the years gone? The memories of the Tavernier days stand out in my mind. Remember how my father would never let me stay overnight, no matter how plastered we were or how late it was? I had to get home that same night.

Then we got married July 5, 1941 and the next time we went to Tavernier I didn't have to go home! It was like being at long last allowed to grow up! I can't remember who else was with us—Jack Mata, for sure, and maybe Mary Hamill. You and Jack said we could use the new little shed you had just built out on the right hand side of the pier. Get the picture—young love, newly married and on a weekend away from it all with NO curfew, and our very own quarters on the Wilkinson's pier in Tavernier... almost the honeymoon we never had! The conditions were absolutely ideal for the newlyweds.

We retired to our suite and settled down to do what, I am sure, most newlyweds do, when the first mosquito struck. The little bastards came up through the cracks in the floor by the droves! We swatted mosquitoes left and right, but they were well organized little devils—they had reinforcements ready for backup attacks... fresh, eager young troops to avenge the ones that had gone before!

Relaxing at the dock.

We tried stuffing the cracks with whatever we could find, but we were outnumbered and out maneuvered. Kay, I will never forget that night as long as I live and we took plenty of ribbing about it the next day from the gang! It was late July and HOT, but we spent the night huddled up in blankets—even our heads—and what sleep we got was to the tune of mosquitoes whining and buzzing and trying to find an opening to the blankets.

All my memories of the "TENT DAYS" are vivid – they had to be or I wouldn't have taken Mel down there for his farewell in 1978. I tried to pick a place where we had been our happiest and our times with you in Tavernier ranked right at the top... both before and after we were married.

I can't forget Johnny running to the Franklin for the gun to shoot the birds, your explanation about the birds being our friends and his reply, "Well, our friends just shit on the pier!"

Or my being out in the boat when a squall came up and Mel running out on the pier to "save" me, missed his footing and fell off and opened up his knee on the rocks. I have never figured out how he was going to save me—I was way out in a boat and he was on the shore with no boat!

The aftermath of that story, however, didn't take place in Tavernier, but rather in Miami Beach when he got subsequent blood poisoning. I got a doctor for him and the doctor told him to use hot compresses on the knee and cold compresses on the

Marie Goecke had her favorite Baby "K" always in sight.

groin. I took my lunch hour from the 3-As to run over to the beach and buy a bag of ice (for which I had to BORROW money) for the compresses, and got back to work.

When I stopped by after work, about 5:30 p.m., I found Charlie Towson and a "Jake" somebody (a crony) sitting in his room drinking highballs. They were using my precious ice in their highballs and were using water from the hotel's water fountain for Mel's groin! I emptied that room in one monumental hurry!

And John, the Dutchman! He never wore socks, but always wore shoes. He was always in the sun and had a permanent tan. When he took off his shoes he looked like he was wearing spats because his feet were pure white!

The "crows nest" was a great place to look over the surroundings.

My introduction to conch chowder was another milestone. You made it in that huge, round pot—a caldron, really—over a wood fire... delicious, pure gourmet. Until then, I didn't even know things even lived in a conch shell—they were just beautiful, ornamental shells that tourists wanted!

And the turtles—and that homemade long-handled prong thing Jack made to rile up the Florida lobsters (so we could catch them) and the water so clear we could watch it happen!

Jack steering the boat—standing up, with two pieces of rope to guide the boat (and a bottle of wine hanging over the side to keep cool). The water looked the same to me in any direction, but he always knew just where he was going and would periodically stop and look down, and sure enough, we would be over a trap, or a coral rock where there were lobsters or something.

I'm getting nostalgic! "K," our times with you, Jack, Johnny and Baby during your "Tent Days" were the highlights of our early years—never, NEVER to be forgotten. I wouldn't trade them for anything.

Old Friends – Mary Lennox (Hamill)

I've lots of happy memories of the Wilkinson's early days in Tavernier. Marie, Mel, Charlie and I were among Jack's AAA gang that sure took advantage of your first home. No doubt Marie's exciting stories include particular details of any I could tell.

However, aside from the wonderful friendship and good times with you – one very vivid memory is how attractive and cozy you made your first home. "K," you had it all so well organized – "a place for everything and everything in its place." It gave one a feeling of being in a separate room – living or kitchen, or bedroom or bath. And everything was so clean and homey. That went for the outside, too – table, benches, all the grounds and docks.

Never having any experience fishing or boating, I always felt very honored when your Jack invited me aboard. What a wealth of knowledge he had – and how patient he was. You were both so gracious and generous letting us invade – hope we didn't leave too much extra mess.

I'm sure Marie has written about our fun at the bar – ??? – sorry I can't remember names, but everyone knew everyone else and it truly was a friendly place. No need for babysitters for you and Jack to join the crowd. I can just visualize either you or Jack ever keeping an eye on Johnny and Katharine sleeping peacefully in your car, parked right beside a window, with the car windows all rolled down – BREEZE AND NO BUGS. Jack's own engineered A/C of a car (B/C War II) was the envy of us all. Remember how even strangers would keep looking at you folks on the road, in mystery?

"K," you can well be proud of the Wilkinson-Mata family contribution to Tavernier life. Just think how valuable your memories are and now present involvement is.

Barracudas

Many people have the wrong impression about barracudas according to the articles that I have read, but some of my old Conch friends who used to go diving into barracudas down near where Cheeca Lodge is now said they weren't afraid of them, but they didn't taunt them.

I think that several of the things that I'd love to tell you about may prove to you that they're really fancy fish that go like lightning. You really need to be aware of them and yet not trust them all the time. The barracuda is one of the most common of the Florida Keys' reef residents. His reputation as a hazard to humans is widespread, yet it may be the most undeserved reputation in the sea. His mouth is overstocked with teeth and he does not mind showing them off. His body resembles a living arrow and he can explode from a motionless pose into lightning speed with unimaginable quickness. Divers who have spent any amount of time in the local waters generally have become used to swimming with barracuda. I know a diver down here who showed us a film that had been taken of him and a particular barracuda that he had gotten friendly with. When he caught a little fish he would go down and hold the piece of fish in his mouth and the barracuda would come and take it out. Talk about brave and daring!

This curious fish is unafraid of humans and it is advisable for divers to react in kind. While it would be foolish to taunt the barracuda, seeing one is certainly no cause for panic. The 'cuda's pointed head is equipped with ample sharp-toothed jaws. Its overall appearance is similar to that of a freshwater pike. The family coloration ranges from dull to bright silver. The belly is white and there are irregular black splotches scattered along its sides. Their dark markings are more numerous near to the tail. Barracuda have an unnerving habit of closely approaching swimmers and divers, however actual attacks are infrequent. Some experts maintain that most encounters stem from the swimmers who have shiny objects such as watches, rings or chains that would clearly attract them and that's what they go for.

In the tent years some of the first fish we got from the dock were barracuda. People would say, "Do you eat barracuda?" We ate them all the time. There were stories about barracuda that came off of the reef having eaten poisonous matter. At times they were noted for being poisonous, but we never found that to be true and we caught many large barracuda off the dock. When we had more fish than we knew what to do with Jack would filet it and salt it down, then hang it in a screen cage that we had on the end of the dock. When there was bad weather we could take out a piece of the fish and soak it and have fish cakes or fry it or have fish stew. It was a wonderful fish to prepare that way because it wasn't flimsy or soft and was firm and really very tasty. We never had any problem with barracuda. It was a good fish to catch, they jump and it's exciting. Many times the kids would throw their lines out and no matter what size barracuda they got they pulled it in. We certainly made good use of everything so there was no stopping us as far as barracuda were concerned.

Robert with freshly caught barracuda on our dock.

Old Friends – Ann and Clint

Dear "K,"

We remember spending one day at your tent site at Planter's Point. You put us up at the "Cistern" motel, accommodations consisted of four cots pushed together, set up in about two or three inches of water. Guests slept with their clothes on, were worried about snakes.

Bathroom privileges were shared. Believe you had a big pail on one side of the tent. Rain water to wash in. Jack took fellows fishing and caught some barracuda and you made a big pot of barracuda stew.

We also remember traveling down to Key West and using the outhouses along the road!

They were the good old days! And we really are so thankful for them.

Love, Ann

Old Friends – Mrs. Tracy

Mrs. Frances Tracy, fondly known as the "Angel of the Keys," soon became a very good friend to Jack and me after our children were born. She was an absolutely fantastic lady and we would sit and talk with her on the front porch of her beautiful home in Tavernier.

After she came to Florida with her husband in 1916 they owned and operated a boat yard in Miami. Fortunately, they survived the terrible 1926 hurricane that destroyed just about everything in the Miami area. She was a real hard worker, working side by side with her husband, who we always called Cap. I think most people referred to him as Captain Roy.

On their vacations they would travel by boat down the Florida Keys to relax and get away from the rat race of running the boat yard. They soon became friends with everyone and they all soon found out that Mrs. Tracy was a nurse. You can believe that anyone with ailments or kids with cuts and bruises would travel to Mrs. Tracy's home. She would do just about anything for anyone. In fact, if she could not take care of their problem she would drive them to Homestead for further treatment and wait to bring them back. She was one in a million.

Even though we had all kinds of medications in the tent, when Jack or I had a cut from a fishhook or something we would always stop to see Mrs. Tracy when we went into Tavernier, to get her okay on what we were doing for it. We learned a lot from her and she used a lot of native plants that date back to Biblical times for medicinal purposes. Aloe was one that we used all the time and Jack would even use it if he had an upset stomach. He would peel the Aloe and put it in a jar of water and let it set. It did the job, but the taste wasn't so great. She had many plants here that she referred to. The gumbo limbo tree was used for a tonic; the leaves would be boiled to make a tea or poultice for a bruise. She came up with things you could hardly believe.

If you had a wasp or bee sting or mosquito bites you had to avoid infection. We would go into Miami to the doctor for pills to give my kids because they would be in the bushes and come out with poison ivy and bug bites, which became infected. There was also sapodilla, which was used for chicle in chewing gum. Another tree was called the bellyache plant or the Barbados Aloe, brought over by

85

the natives from the Bahamas in 1865. It was a treat to visit her as she was always telling us something new so we would make excuses just to come by and see her.

Once the Overseas Highway was opened and more people came down here it was evident we needed a doctor, someone who would stay here. Mrs. Tracy and Commissioner Harry Harris got together with Doc Lowe, a very smart Conch who was in real estate and who had been here for many years, and Paul Burcham and Hurt McLean, two young men who were very active in starting the Key Largo Civic Club. Doc Lowe was called Doc because he would give first aid to folks who came to him. Thelma Cooper, a nurse who worked very hard over the years, and Lottie Huey, also a nurse, volunteered their services and in 1952 the Tavernier Medical Center was opened. Between them, Mrs. Tracy and Harry Harris were able to convince Dr. Harvey Cohn of Victoria Hospital in Miami to come down and work in the clinic and he was absolutely a God send. The clinic was very successful.

We had many good times over the years with Mrs. Tracy. She helped with the Coral Shores School and was very active with the Key Largo Garden Club, which they dedicated and which is known as the Mrs. Tracy Garden Club. She had the project of supervising the school landscaping and maintenance. I remember my mother living here with my grandmother in a little cottage behind Mrs. Tracy and helping her to supervise. It really makes one feel good that over the years these older folks had so much interest in and did so much for this little community.

After we started the American Legion Auxiliary, Mrs. Tracy was one of the first people to receive the Community Service Award. I was President at the time and it was a treat for me because I remembered all the things that she did that she would never take anything for. She never wanted to be compensated. She was just a people person and loved doing it. Many a night she would go to the bedside of a woman having a baby, helping as if she was a doctor. She was really an angel to do so much for so many.

Before she came to the Keys she was very active in the founding of Jackson Memorial Hospital and Variety Children's Hospital. Always active in her nursing field even though she worked so hard with her husband in the boat yard, she was very smart and worked in the public health area in Miami. When she did her nurses' training at John Hopkins, she volunteered her services with the Army during the Spanish American War. She was very talented and had a great deal of experience with health facilities and never lost her touch.

When my daughter Katharine graduated from Florida State, Mrs. Tracy gave her the pin she had received when she finished nurses training and Katharine had it made into a charm. Before that, she gave my son Johnny the silver loving cup she had received when she was a child. You can see Mrs. Tracy was very dear to us.

Captain Roy was a dyed-in-the-wool Republican; he and my Jack hit it off fine and they would talk about all their fishing escapades. He was quite a talker and they would be off in the corner of the porch and Mrs. Tracy would then tell us several little stories. She said when they first started coming to the Keys it was really wild, and I mean wild! There weren't many people around and everything was hit and miss. The railroad was still in operation in the 1920s and she said the crews were rough and raw, the dregs of humanity. A woman wasn't safe alone and since she had places to go to treat someone who was sick she couldn't be scared of her own shadow. It would be in the middle of the night and you never knew when you would come across one of these guys, not knowing who they were or what they would do. She always carried a pistol in her belt, and she knew how to use it. A few times she thought she might have to, but she never did.

The stories she told about the Keys and her life made our trips interesting so when we found her at home we could corner her just to hear them and have some limeade. It was such a treat. Here I was from the big city of Philadelphia, so it was very foreign and exciting to me.

Captain Roy Tracy would come down and help Jack load the tropical fish he caught for Marine Studios. He'd be right there by the dock like a sidewalk superintendent. He knew a lot about fish, but he hadn't seen much of these colorful fish and he enjoyed it so much. He became ill and died in 1965 at the ripe old age of 87. Mrs. Tracy then moved into a little house by Cliff Carpenter's and lived there for five years. She died in 1970 at the age of 93 and was buried near her family in Delaware. A plaque hangs in the Garden Center that bears her name and proclaims her "The Angel of the Keys." She certainly was, and we loved her dearly.

Sharks

There are some shark facts that I think are important. With as many sharks as we used to catch, we only caught them for Jack to cut them open for the liver, which we boiled for oil. When the weather was a little rough or inclement, we could go out on the boat and throw this oil out and it would make the water just as clear as

anything. With the glass bottom bucket we could then see the ledges where we wanted to get crawfish or certain kinds of fish that Jack liked, yellowtail or grouper, so we weren't stuck on shore. This oil was very important, but it smelled to high heaven so we had to be very careful that we didn't spill it on ourselves or in the boat because it was a real mess to get out of your clothes.

Now, when I look back I find there are some interesting facts that I've saved in my scrapbooks. It says that the image of sharks being villains lurking around beaches to devour luckless swimmers still appears to be fiction. Florida residents and tourists should learn to distinguish between the two. The facts say that the risk of being killed by a shark is reportedly less than that of being killed by a bee sting. Some sharks are so small, six inches, that even when grown they pose no threat to man. In Florida, only one swimmer in 5,000,000 has been bothered by a shark. The number of documented serious shark attacks on people has averaged 26 worldwide in recent years (this is from back 20 years ago). Man is not part of the shark's natural diet and only a few

Jack would cut out the shark's liver, then boil it and use the oil to clear the water to see the bottom so he could find his crawfish ledges and fish holes.

species have ever been proven to have attacked man. Every shark, however, should be considered potentially dangerous.

Johnny protecting Katharine –
she did not know the shark was dead.

*The kids loved it when we
pulled in a big one.*

The main population of sharks is found offshore in deeper water. Experts with knowledge say that the intelligence of sharks is low while their sense of smell is very keen. In fact, experts say sharks never could have outlasted dinosaurs without keen senses. The shark is nature's vacuum cleaner. Soft drink bottles, tin cans, magazines, old clothes, anchors, boat propellers, lead sinkers, and even logs have been found in sharks' stomachs.

In spite of its appetite for junk food, the shark is considered by scientists to be a valuable animal in research on cancer and aging. Sharks also offer a variety of products that have commercial potential. For example, shark is an excellent seafood, shark liver provides oil, shark hides are tanned as high-grade leather and the jaws and teeth are sold as curios. The smallest known shark is the dwarf shark, which measures about six inches when fully grown. The largest is the whale shark, which can grow up to 60 feet long and weigh several tons. Most sharks have no oceanic enemies or predators except other sharks.

There is one shark recipe that I thought would be interesting to repeat. I think back to all the sharks we caught and little did we know then that one day shark would be considered a real appetizer and be used in so many ways. The flesh of the preferred species of shark is pure white. Because the shark's skeletal structure is made of cartilage, cleaning and butchering of the boneless meat for market and table are easily accomplished and cooking is simple. Shark, like all fish, is a highly nutritious meal, a complete protein food with B vitamins, thiamin, riboflavin and niacin. Atlantic mako, considered by many to be the best tasting of all sharks, has a texture and flavor comparable to the more expensive swordfish. Ranking along with the mako are the hammerheads, lemon, bonnet head, sharp-nose and black sharks, all considered excellent in flavor. The dog fish or pound shark is considered a prize catch. Filets are white and firm with a flaky texture similar to the popular haddock. I never dreamed, in this day and age, we would be interested in sharks, but apparently as we grow older we become wiser about many of the things we once threw away because of old stories about them. It's great to know that

K pulling in a shark early in the morning.

there are so many more things in the ocean that we can enjoy and are good for us. We would save the skull; there was a good one hanging over the front of our tent and I have several in my home now and they bring back memories of the sharks we used to catch and throw away. So anybody reading this remember not to throw your sharks away, they can be used for many things as well as food. That's just another little tidbit I have added to my memories.

I found a recipe for baked Florida shark with mushrooms that sounds great and is something you could add to your cookbook. A pound and a half of Florida shark filets, either fresh or frozen, half teaspoon of salt, quarter teaspoon of pepper, a cup of sliced mushrooms, half cup condensed cream of celery soup, a quarter cup of dry white wine and one cup of grated sharp cheddar cheese, parsley to garnish. Thaw if frozen, skin filets, cut into several serving portions. Place in a single layer in well-greased one-and-a-half quart shallow casserole, sprinkle with salt and pepper, combine mushrooms, soup and wine, spread over fish, sprinkle with cheese, cover and bake at 350 degrees for 20-25 minutes or until the fish is flaky; test with a fork. It makes four servings. The next time you get shark treat yourself to a nice meal.

Jack works cleaning a shark.

"Look what I caught!"

A Typical Day in Planter

We were early risers and on a typical day in Planter we would get up and have a good breakfast first thing. Usually it was grapefruit and sometimes eggs and grits and bacon, if we were lucky enough to have it. We were not coffee drinkers, so we'd have juice or something of that sort. Then we'd get in the skiff and go out fishing for the day. Maybe we'd come across a turtle or we might see a stingray that Jack just wanted to tease. Jack had several places where he'd like to go fishing; we'd use nothing but hand lines in those days and anyway they seemed to be the best. Time just seemed to drift by and we weren't in a hurry to go anywhere or do anything.

There was one special place that we liked because we could get the crawfish that we wanted; we didn't take any more than we needed. There was a ledge right off what is now Harry Harris Park. We'd have a tickler and would tickle it just enough to get out a couple to have when we went home. When the weather was nice we could do that, but couldn't if it was too rough. We'd just mosey around and it seemed that time just went by. We'd go out around Tavernier Key and find different spots out there to anchor and catch a few yellowtail or grunts. Then we'd wander on home and by that time we were ready to have a snack of some sort.

We'd change our clothes and walk into town because we didn't have a car at that time. It was a mile to the highway and a mile more to Tavernier. Our big thing of the day was getting mail and of course my mother wanted to hear from me. It seemed that somehow or other I did write a letter every day. What I found to say I don't know, other than the weather and the fish that we caught and just being there and enjoying it. It was such an uncluttered life. We didn't have to worry about telephones or anybody knocking on the door to sell us something. Of course, we didn't have to worry too much about the heat, we were always very comfortable. If it did get windy or anything we could always put the sides of the tent down, so that wasn't any problem. Sometimes we were lucky enough to get a hunk of ice and if it didn't melt too much by the time we wandered on home we put it in this little ice box we had. It didn't keep the ice too long, but it was good enough for the cold things that we wanted.

We'd usually have our big meal around four o'clock so we'd be inside before the mosquitoes took over. Jack was an avid reader and I would catch up on my mail and other little projects that I wanted to do. Each day just seemed to be better than the one before. It was a real treat just being there together and I was enjoying all these outdoor activities. I liked sitting on the dock when he was out looking around for different places for fish.

When our friends came down they were amazed and they couldn't believe that Jack knew where all the fish were, but he had all these markers on his line. At times he would joke with different ones and say, "Yeah, you have to mark them on the side of the boat when you find a new one." They kind of looked at him like he was crazy. He said, "Well, that's one way to tell where it is."

The days seemed to fly by and it was just wonderful. If it rained hard we had many projects to do inside and that was when Jack read about so many things. Later on in the evening we had the big bonfire and smudge pots if the mosquitoes or sand flies were too bad. It was just such a pleasure to sit outside and enjoy the stars. He tried to teach me a lot about the stars, which of course went in one ear and out the other, but it was beautiful anyway. I tried to appear interested, which I really was, but I wouldn't know one from the other today. It made good conversation, anyway. When I think about

him I remember he had so many things he would talk about. Then the Thompson brothers would join us and it was just an easy way to take each day as it came.

One thing about Jack, he never discriminated. One of his good friends was a black man named Racket who lived a block or two behind us back in the bushes. He took care of his wife, who was blind, and he was so dear to her. He worked on the railroad years ago and then afterwards he did odd jobs for people in Tavernier so he made enough to keep food on the table for his wife. I remember when Jack was in the service and came home to see us, Racket would

Time for a cool one!

94

always call him Captain Jack. He was only a lieutenant then, so he would say Captain Lieutenant and it was cute. He was so fond of Jack because he treated him like a real friend, which he truly was.

One thing Jack always did say was that he liked to stay put and not keep moving around, so I guess in this way he was happy that I agreed to be here with him so that we wouldn't have to move. It just seemed that each day that went by was better than the one before and we were just happy to be together. Eventually we did get to meet different people. I know it was a year before Jack really took me into town to meet anyone, but he had met any number of people. They called me a "prisoner of love" because they didn't know what I was like and where I came from. They did know my name; he had fun with that.

Many times I didn't want to go into town, but after he conned his mother out of this air-cooled Franklin in which he put screens, we could go back and forth without being eaten alive. When it rained, and of course it was all wetlands where we were with big holes and lots of rocks, he would carry me piggy back into town because he didn't want me to get my feet wet and catch cold and have to go back to Philadelphia. So whatever it was, he had a way of making sure that I was comfortable and that each day was better than the last one. That would be typical of a day we had in Planter, and of course as I look back it was really great.

Stingrays

Jack used to catch stingrays for the Marine Studios in St. Augustine, but they were very difficult to tie up and keep until the trucks came down to get the specimens. He had to get a license to do this because some of the fish were very unusual or delicate. We would go out in the skiff for the stingrays. I would steer the motor and we would track them down. He would strike them in the wing tip so it wouldn't hurt the animal itself and bring it into the boat. He'd put a rope through the back of the gills and that is how we were able to tie them up at the dock that night. Hopefully the next day they would still be alive, because there wasn't any other way we could keep them in a trap for the marine studios. We'd try to catch a ray just before they were going to come down and pick it up. On several occasions when we pulled the rope in we found a shark had come and taken a big hunk out of it during the night and of course killed it. So we weren't that lucky in saving them for the studios, but it was another sport that we enjoyed and it was fun anyway.

The newborn rays are practically identical to their parents except for their face, in that when born they are on a one/twelfth scale. While the pup measures about five inches across, the full grown southern stingray may reach five feet in width. Like the parents, the young are born with their distinctive stinger in the tail.

A beautiful ray.

The rays are not normally aggressive towards man, but a wader or swimmer may find himself in an unpleasant encounter with a stingray in the wild. Stingrays, like most members of their family, often bury themselves in sand. When this happens in shallow water an unwary bather may find himself stepping on a piece of bottom that suddenly moves. When stopped the ray flexes the whips and with his slender tail continues the stinger forward and into his attacker. The sting from the ray can be painful and the wound should be cleaned as soon as possible with medical attention following soon afterwards.

Johnny with a half-eaten ray, very interesting pose.

If you are stung by a ray, the stinger goes in but you cannot pull it out. It breaks off of the animal and it must be cut out, which is very painful and dangerous. That is why you must have medical attention right away. Waders can usually avoid contact with a ray by shifting their feet along the bottom when they walk. This will scare

Stingrays, very interesting sealife, but very hard to keep alive.

off any rays that happen to be dozing in their path. They love to sun and hide under the sand so sharks or anything else cannot find them.

The southern stingrays are most common in an area from the Caribbean to North Carolina. Like all rays, they are closely related to the sharks. They have skeletons like the sharks, with cartilage rather than bone, and both have five pairs of gill openings. Unlike sharks, rays do not have teeth designed to rip and tear. The southern stingray forages for crabs, shrimp and other small fish by using its wings to stir up the bottom and reveal the burrowing species. They're very exciting animals to see, but they are very hard to catch and keep. We enjoyed our experiences with them and have many pictures in our album. This was just another phase of sea life and my life in the tent with Jack, a wonderful fisherman who knew so much about all the sea creatures.

Jack Was a Good Mother

I never believed how attentive a father Jack would be until we had Johnny. He was born near Philadelphia where we were staying with my folks. There was just nothing that Jack wouldn't do for me when we brought Johnny back to the tent.

The first day home we put a board outside with a towel on it and that's where we were going to give him his first bath. We had warmed the water and had soap and towels and everything handy. He came over and I said, "I'm going to bathe the baby and then later maybe we'll go out in the boat or whatever."

He said, "Oh, no. I'm going to help you."

I said, "What do you mean?'

He said, "Well, you can bathe him from the waist up and I will bathe him from the waist down."

"Well," I said, "Okay if you want to, this will be a together thing anyway. You're the daddy and I'm the momma." So we just had the best time soaping him up and I guess he never realized just how attentive we were with him.

However, that was just one of the things that was always so good. Jack washed all the diapers. He got water out of the cistern and made a big fire. He boiled the diapers on the fire in this big tub and hung them out and when they were dry he would fold them up and put them in the house. In those days we didn't have the disposable kind, just the cotton ones, which were so nice anyway.

During the day when we'd go out to the end of the dock he would hold him because he didn't trust me—I might fall overboard, even though Johnny would be in his basket. We would go out there and just enjoy the sea breeze, giving him a little bit of sunshine. We knew that we couldn't do too much because he would get sunburned, but we did want him to get used to it because this was where he was going to live. Anyway, we just wanted to do things together.

One evening I went on to bed as I was pretty tired and thought I would sleep like a log. During the night Johnny cried and Jack got up and changed his diaper and brought him to me to nurse. He thought it wouldn't take too long before he got a belly full. It seemed he was eating every two hours because Jack was a good one for believing that if the baby cries it means he's hungry or he wants his diaper changed. It wasn't unlike Jack to say why doesn't he go to sleep—he's already been fed. He changed his diaper and put him back in the little basket. Just a couple of hours later he cried again. Jack said, "Darn it, he can't be that hungry." He would get back up and change his diaper and bring him to me again. When he thought he had enough he changed his diaper again and put him back in the basket. Before long, another hour at the most, he started crying again and Jack said, "What on earth is wrong?" He thought maybe he needed to be burped or had colic or something. He changed him again and patted him, thinking if he did have colic or needed to burp maybe it would come up.

Well it didn't, so he gave him another chance and when Johnny got to nursing he said, "Listen you little bastard, this is one time you're going to get your belly full." He put his little feet up and he tickled the bottom of his feet enough to keep him awake because he just wanted to be in bed with us and sleep, it was so nice and cozy. When he got hungry it was right there, there was no place to go and no hurry. He kept him awake until he knew he must have had a belly full, then back in his basket he went.

Before long it was morning. I was never an early riser anyway. When I turned over I said, "Wasn't it great, Johnny didn't get up once during the night and I had a good night's sleep."

He said, "The hell he did, the little bastard, god damn it, I was up with him three different times." I never knew. "No, you sleep so hard he could cry his eyes out all night and you wouldn't know it, but I took care of him."

So, you see, he was very attentive and he just loved it really. It was one thing he could bitch about and tell people that he was the one that got up and did all the work, which of course didn't make me mad anyway. But, I know over the years he was always very attentive, he was a very devoted father. When Katharine came along he had his time with her, too. So it was always tit for tat who was going to do what for whom. Over the

This big jewfish makes Johnny look like a midget.

years, as I look back, I think that's one reason why he was absolutely crushed when he was drafted, because he was going to have to leave me and the children.

Here he was 34 years old with two kids, but we were just beachcombers and he was not a Conch so they just decided well out you go boy, so that was the end of that. But after the war when he came back, the times we had were just great and I just can't say enough about the devotion he had. He truly loved the family life and little did I know when we first got married that he would have that kind of deep love. I guess that's one reason why, when I look back on them, the five years we lived in the tent were probably the five greatest years that I've had.

Johnny and Katharine in Paradise, And Then Came Robert

Little did I know when I came down here to live in a tent that I would have two children to bring up in the uncluttered paradise of clean, open air with wonderful seafood and nothing to bother us. Just to get up and be happy you were alive was wonderful.

Johnny was born outside of Philadelphia. I had to go up and stay there for a couple of months before he was born in September of 1928. When we brought him back down here my mother nearly had a fit. She tried to talk the doctor into telling us we couldn't come down here where we didn't have any doctors or hospitals or anything around in case the baby got sick. Where would we go and what would we do? To make a long story short, we just listened and yessed them to death and we came back anyway.

Our beginning years with Johnny as a baby were really so beautiful you just couldn't believe it. We were right there on the water and we carried him around in a basket until he could walk. Jack would take us out in the skiff and we'd mosey around to find turtles or fish or crawfish or conchs just to get out. Of course we had an umbrella that we put over Johnny in the skiff so he didn't get too much sun. As he got older Jack built a screened room off the end of the dock and put a tarp over it that somebody gave us. We could put him in there anytime. When we had guests come out to visit we would sit out on the end of the dock just talking and having fun and

Screened-in room off to the right of the dock.

102

he was in the screened room. Out of the sun, not running up and down the dock and falling overboard, which we did worry about because he did it many times. It didn't seem to worry him too much, though, and eventually he learned to swim on his own. It got to the point where he liked being under the water more than being on the top, but at first he hated to get his face wet; other than that, he didn't mind getting wet.

As time went on we got him a little trap that he could hang over the end of the dock. When the tide came in, bringing seaweed and everything with it, he would get bunches of seaweed from along the shoreline and shake them out. He'd get the prettiest little shrimp or sargassum fish and he would put them in his little trap. He would pick up shells along the shoreline and he kept pretty busy. He never seemed to worry about toys because he was so intrigued with all the things that were around, ants and crabs and whatever. When we came back from fishing it was time for him to take a nap.

After Jack conned his mother out of the air-cooled Franklin and screened the windows we would go into town and check the mail and get ice and other things we needed. In the meantime, we had made several friends and it was a real treat to go into town. When we got back it was time to have our big meal and settle down for the evening before the mosquitoes came. After that it was a ritual for the Thompson brothers to come over, especially in the wintertime when it was a little cool. It was such a treat to have a fire and those were the times when they would tell us about the good old days and about Planter and when they lived in Key West. Each day was prettier than the one before and we were just happy to be there, taking it easy.

K and Jack and the Franklin with the screened windows.

It wasn't too long before I got pregnant with Katharine and by that time my folks had moved back to Coral Gables. They would come down to visit with us in the tent and make sure everything was okay with Johnny. They were just amazed that we had everything under control and there was nothing they had to worry about. Many times they would try to talk me into letting them take Johnny up for a weekend, but I would never let them, except when we had to go up to see the baby doctor and they would come down and get me.

It was so funny. The doctor would say, "God, Kay, the bottom of this kid's feet are like leather." Of course he went barefoot all the time and didn't seem to worry about going over the rocks, it was just natural to him. When I first got him a pair of little sandals it was like shodding a horse. He would try to kick them off and it was a riot. He didn't want anything, he wanted to be barefoot and that was that. After I became pregnant with Katharine I would let the folks take Johnny just for a weekend to give me a break.

Katharine was born at Victoria Hospital in Miami and that was another story. "Now you've got two babies, now what are you going to do?" "Well," I said, "the same thing I have been doing, what's the difference?" So we came back to the tent and we had a crib for Johnny and had Katharine in the same basket, which we put on top of the little kitchen table. We were very cozy, but we had plenty of room. Of course I nursed her so there wasn't any problem with refrigeration or formulas or anything of that sort.

Jack was good about taking them out in the boat.

Johnny would race up and down the dock like you couldn't believe. He had his little fishing line that kept him busy during the day. I remember one time Jack was trying to catch a bonefish just up the shoreline and we had to be very quiet. I was in the tent doing something with Katharine and all of a sudden I heard Johnny holler at Jack, "Hey you old son of a bitch, who ever told you you could fish?" With that Jack threw his fishing line down and he started after Johnny. Johnny ran into the

104

bushes. Jack said, "You little bastard, when you come out you know what you're going to get. You're never to holler at me like that." But Jack should have remembered all the times Johnny was out fishing with him when Katharine and I couldn't go because she was too young. Later on when we all went out in the skiff with the equipment, poles, spears and the glass bottom bucket there was hardly room for the four of us, but we managed. We had everything under control.

Finally, when Johnny came out he got a good whipping. I said to Jack afterwards, "You know, that's not fair. He goes fishing with you so much and when you miss something you cuss. He's a smart little kid and he picks up all of this and knows how to use it so you better watch it. Of course we'll reprimand him too, but then he'll say, "Daddy does it, so what's the difference?"

We had a big tub that we would fill with water and the kids would play in it. When Katharine was still small, Johnny liked to splash in there with her and get her all wet and make her scream. It was just great the way you could improvise and still have everything

They loved swimming in a big tub.

just about the way it should be. As Katharine grew older and could race around and walk pretty well, she was barefoot too, of course. They had on their little dungaree outfits and I would give them each a jar with holes in the lid. Up the shoreline they would go, collecting all kinds of ants and spiders and who knows what all. In those days we didn't have plastic and I never even thought that they might fall and break the jar and could have cut themselves and bled to death. I just sent them off and trusted in the Dear Lord and he took care of them. Before long they came back with the little jars full of spiders that had intertwined with one of the webs and ants and you can't imagine what all. Of course, I took the lids off to get rid of those things and, oh, they screamed at me. Johnny said, "No way, they're

*Kathy loved the dock and we
always had to watch her.*

my friends." He also had a pocket full of bull ants. I can't imagine why they never did sting him, but they sure did sting me. I said, "No way, you can't keep them." He said, "Well, they're my friends." I said, "Well, friend or not, they're stinging me and that's the end of that, so let's not worry about it."

Often when we went into Tavernier Johnny would be sleeping on cushions on the back seat of the Franklin and Katharine would be in the little basket. We would visit with our friends and with the screens we didn't have to worry about the bugs biting them. We'd go to Janice's house for a fish fry and they were so pleased to have made friends and have us be there, part of their family. Many times we would go to the old drug store where Evelyn Allen would come and play the piano. McKenzie and Ralph Lund were there with their instruments and Marty McKinney and Bud were quite the singers. We'd get together and just have a wonderful Saturday night; this was our night out.

*Great grandma Keifer loved
watching the kids.*

Yvonne and Broomie took care of the drug store and McKenzie owned it. We'd have wonderful times and we didn't have to worry about the kids because they were locked up in the car. They had plenty of food and Katharine was taking the bottle so every time they'd cry someone would go out. I'd give each one of them a turn to look and see if the

106

babies were okay and sure enough they were fine.

We had our evenings out so we weren't confined completely to the tent and yet it didn't bother us. Our friends in Tavernier were so nice and they just enjoyed coming and visiting with us. It reminded them of the good old days when there wasn't anything around and most of their time was spent fishing and swimming.

Yvonne was the one who told me of the many times they swam with all the barracudas when they lived in Islamorada where Cheeca Lodge is now and she said they never bothered them. When I think about the barracudas and how much we enjoyed them, I

K and more good fishing!

always think of Yvonne diving in among them. As long as you don't bother them, they don't bother you. So all the little things that I learned along the way were true; it all came from the Conch people and that was one thing I never did question.

Five years went by and the war came along. Jack was drafted, one of the first from Monroe County. He was 34 years old and had two children, but we were just beach combers. We were not Conchs, we were not natives, so he was among the first and he led the troops from

Monroe County when they came through Tavernier in a big bus. Everybody was out there crying because there were a couple of our old timers along with him. It was just the idea that we'd had two children and he was at that age when you would think he would not be called. That meant that I could not stay in the tent because there was no way I could live there by myself.

I didn't drive so that was when we had to move to Coral Gables and live with my mother, grandmother, my brother, his wife and my two sisters. In those days, houses were hard to find because the Emory Riddle School was teaching some of the soldiers to fly. Here we were, five families living in one house. I think my poor grandmother had to sleep on the couch. My mother was working then for the army as an interpreter because she could speak Spanish. I was left to do the grocery shopping and I'd have to get the bus, taking Katharine and Johnny with me. I'd get the groceries and take the bus back and fortunately it left me off on the corner just across the street from where we lived. The kids would take turns carrying the groceries across and we always seemed to manage.

With my mother working all week she felt so sorry for the rest of us that on the weekends she would try to take us for a ride or out to eat so at least we got away from the house, especially for my grandmother who ended up having to do all the cooking and everything for us. My kids just loved shrimp, they were not hot dog or hamburger eaters. Being raised on the Keys with all the seafood around, naturally we didn't have that kind of food around very much. We would enjoy the ride up A1A, looking at the water and trees. One place in Hollywood where we always stopped had wonderful seafood. Mother would drop us at the door and go to park the car. We would get a booth because it was more comfortable for all of us with Grandmother and the kids, and Katharine was in a high chair.

While we were waiting for the food to come Johnny was always very talkative. He used to stand up and lean over the booth and talk to the people behind us. In conversation he said, "Well, hi, what are you bastards going to have today for lunch?" I thought I would die. I pulled him around and down and said, "Don't you ever say that and don't you ever talk to anybody unless you can be nice." I said to my mother, "This is the last time that we bring these children out." Poor darling Katharine could hardly talk; Johnny did all the talking for her. I said, "Here we go again, Johnny using all the words he learned from his father." When I told Jack this story he really cracked up.

There was a little nursery school the kids went to, but after two years of that I said to hell with this. Johnny and Katharine had five bosses. When you're living like that, so close, everything you do is wrong. The kids got on the family's nerves and we were all confined. We couldn't let them go outside alone as they weren't used to cars or anything like that. I met some friends next door, he was in the navy and his wife had a little baby so my kids had somebody to play with. I said, "I've got to go back to the Keys." It wasn't too long afterwards that he said he would be happy to drive me down. I packed up his car, he brought me to Tavernier, I got a little house and that is where I was when Jack got out of the service one year later.

I told Jack, "You can divorce me or you can do anything you want, but the city life with these kids is not for me." Even though, I

Katharine and Johnny – cute – cute- cute!

appreciated having a place to go while Jack was gone. He was in Italy for three years so when he came back, I had been down here a year by myself, taking care of the kids, but it hadn't been a problem. It was just another stage of my life and we handled it and didn't worry about it. Of course, I had already made friends with my Conch associates down here so they were there to help me. I could walk to the store so I didn't have to worry about not driving and it's surprising what you can do when you have to. It was very pleasant and of course my family would come down to visit. They couldn't believe that I would stay down there all alone without anyone around, but it didn't make any difference and before too long Jack was home.

We got a bigger house in Tavernier and then he had a couple of jobs. He worked for the electric company and then was with the

mosquito control commission. At one time he was going to be a boat fisherman, but after a while that didn't work out too well. It was too confining and he just wanted to be with us more. It wasn't too long before I got pregnant with Robert and I always said Robert was my coming-home present. Johnny was then six and Katharine was five, so I had another baby and he was the apple of our eye.

Robert after the tent days.

Johnny and Katharine would fight to help change Robert's diapers and take care of him so I had two babysitters and that was just great. The kids grew up here and they all graduated from Coral Shores School. I became very involved in the Parent Teachers Association and also in the American Legion Auxiliary and then of course with planning for the new Coral Shores High School. My kids did very well.

We trapped coons and caged them 'till we were hungry and tired of seafood.

When Johnny graduated he joined the Navy at 18 and was in for four years. Katharine graduated from Coral Shores High School the next year and she went to Florida State for four years and became a teacher. When Robert graduated he hadn't made the grades that would get him into college. I told him that his father always said the Navy was the best service and rather than wait till he might be drafted I thought the best thing for him to do was to go into the Navy. At the time, he didn't think much of the idea, but he was only 17. I said, "You're not going to hang around the Keys doing nothing and we don't have the money to try to get you into college." In the meantime, Jack had gotten another job over in the islands with the Army. It was a civilian job and with his education and experience he did very well, but I was left again with the three kids. I took Robert and signed him up for the Navy and he was in for three years. He volunteered for Vietnam and he was over there the whole time.

So the kids all turned out fine. They grew up here in the Keys and there was nothing wrong with living this country life. Each one married and had a family and they have all been very dear to me. I have seven grandkids and now I have four great-grandchildren. My life has been pretty full and looking back on it, it's been just wonderful. I don't know what I would have done without my children; they have given me more children to be with and be proud of. I guess that's the way life goes and I am always thankful that I'm still here enjoying the Keys. It's now 1996 and it's taken me a long time to get this story put together, but at 80 I hope I have a few more years to be here in the only place I want to be.

Remembering

It's February 1996 now and as I look back I realize that in December I will have been here in the Keys for 60 years. I have been so lucky, having those five years in the tent and so many wonderful friends who came to visit and who have shared their comments and memories with you. It meant a lot to me because it helped me to complete my story. It seems that each one, as they come back, say, "Are you still here?" I say, "Yes, by golly, by the grace of God I am."

Jack was always a great one for saying "become involved" and after the war I was very active in the Parent Teachers Association. Then, I worked to get the bond issue to build the Coral Shores High School, which took us three years, but we won. We're now in the process of getting a new high school as we've outgrown this one because the Keys have grown so much. As I look back, I feel very honored to have been awarded a PTA Life Membership.

So many people tell me I should write about what I've done through my involvement in the community. My purpose in life was the education of the children and when I did get a job I was the first secretary and then Office Manager of Coral Shores School for 26 years, so I was more than involved with the school.

I became very active with the American Cancer Society and have been a volunteer for 24 years with them. Over the years, I never realized how involved I was until 1975 when the Monroe County Kiwanians honored the first ten outstanding citizens in Monroe County. I was the first woman named along with nine men in those first ten people and of course I was more than honored. My family was there and they were just as flabbergasted as I was.

I've been a member of the Daughters of the American Revolution since 1943 and they presented me with a community service award two years ago. I was the Organizing Regent here in 1983. The Rotarians made me an Honorary Rotarian and that was a real treat, I tell you. They presented me with a beautiful plaque because of my involvement in the community and all the things I have done. Being an Honorary Rotarian has been a very special honor for me.

The "Monroe County Florida Keys Room" in the Hope Lodge was dedicated in 1992. With the help of organizations and citizens in the community, I was able to raise $28,000 to fund this

111

project. I was honored with a "Distinguished Service Award" for the state from the Florida Division of the American Cancer Society for 42 years of volunteer service and named "Outstanding Volunteer" in 1993 by the Upper Keys Unit.

I was the first woman to be grand Marshall of the Reporter's 4th of July Parade and Grand Marshall in 1977 for the high school's Thanksgiving Day Parade. Several years ago the Jaycees named me the Outstanding Senior Citizen of the Upper Keys. I feel that I'm bragging, but I don't mean to. I'm just a doer and not one to sit back. My family has been great and my seven grandchildren and now four great-grandchildren are all just so wonderful to me. I have been a widow now for 18 years. It's just wonderful to think of the life that I have had and I am just so grateful for all those people who were a part of it. The memories will last forever.

I think now of things that I have forgotten to say, but my life has been so full and I thank everyone who has contributed to my happiness and helped me to do the things I was able to do. I feel like I've lived a long time. I just became 80 this year and it scares the hell out of me, but in the meantime I'm going to keep moving and doing what I can, particularly with the Cancer Society. This is the time for me to say thanks to everybody for making my life so rich and so great and hopefully I'll have a few more years to do as much as I possibly can.

Remembering With Love

When I awoke this morning I called your name.
  I waited for your answer, it never came
I listened for a telltale sound...
  The silence of stillness was all I found.

Then I remembered you were no longer here.
  In my mind however, you will always be near.
From my heart you will never be gone.
  Yet, everyone says I must move on.

I'll always remember the good times now past.
  I dwell on those memories, they will always last.
I think about the kindness that was always you.
  I remember the little things you used to do.

I always felt safe, you were strong with life.
  I was always proud to be your wife.
I thank God for His many gifts divine.
  I'll always be thankful He made you mine.

I trust you now rest in His peace and care.
  Only He loved you as I did, my dear.
When this day is over and at its end...
  I sleep with the dreams of my husband and friend.

by Richard R. LaMarra

It Had To Be You

It had to be you,
It had to be you.
I wandered around
And finally found
The somebody who,
Could make me be true,
Could make me feel blue.
Even to be glad,
Just to be sad,
Thinking of you.

Some others I've seen,
Might never be mean.
Might never be cross,
Or try to be boss,
But they wouldn't do.

Cause nobody else gives me a thrill,
With all your faults I love you still.

It had to be you,
Wonderful you,
It had to be you.

© 1924 Kahn and Jones

Dancing at Donnie's Bayshore
Beer and Restaurant in
Tavernier –
25th Wedding Anniversary.

Made in the USA
Columbia, SC
24 September 2019